David Davenport

Teshuvah
David's Key

David A. Davenport

Table of Contents

Preface

Each of us born in the Western Hemisphere is subsequently born-into an existence which can, at this stage in history, generally be observed-as and defined-by wanton consumerism and the perpetual quest for self-gratification. True, we must consume, to simply survive, however we also possess the innate predisposition at this stage to amass and squander things, *far beyond* our primordial needs. As well, we are predisposed to manipulating fellow human beings in this quest for self-gratification. It is then generally not until we exit childhood, and perhaps as we transition to early adulthood that we begin to become acquainted with a subtle gnawing in our souls, a spiritual void which is often ignored and suppressed for many years, if not an entire lifetime.

Until we come to terms with this void and realize that we were designed to daily commune with God, and to recognize His voice as would a sheep its shepherd; that we live lives of vanity and self-service; consuming time, space and matter; while also storing-up the same for our progeny—that *they* may in turn do the same—a perpetual cycle of consuming and amassing temporal things—none of which will accompany us in the hereafter—the eternal. We thus serve and feed an endless cycle of vanity. Perhaps King Solomon, in Ecclesiastes 1:14, was surly onto something as he stated, *"I have seen all the works that are done under the sun, and behold, all is vanity and striving after wind."* Indeed, "all is vanity"—when "all" is not centered upon a life of daily intimacy with Jesus.

To be sure, we can occasionally shine, perhaps through humanitarian feats, committing noble and charitable acts; but such typically feeds only the temporal, and does little to impact the *eternal*—when it is not rendered for the glory of God—and when it is not sown with the *love* of God.

It is only when we embrace God as the center of our personal universe that the soul begins to feed upon the daily provision of a heavenly manna in the form of divine guidance, illumination, inspiration and affirmation, each step of the way. It is herein that we are transformed, atom-by-atom, into beings, which then carryout noble and charitable acts on a daily basis—noble and charitable acts adorned with the love of God. It is *then,* that these acts impact the eternal.

The vast majority of people living in the western hemisphere are equally born-into relative comfort, security and stability, as compared to nations and cultures bereft of the freedoms (albeit freedoms violently under attack at present) in the West. For these, it is with ease that they may sail through childhood and early adulthood relatively free of trauma—trauma to the soul. For a smaller percentage of us; comfort, security and stability are foreign conditions. Rather, fear, anxiety, pain, rejection, depression, isolation, confusion, despondency and despair are the order of the day— ingredients that can become such an integral part of our beings that we can hardly recognize the blue in the sky, or the warmth of the sun, though they both stare us in the face. For these there beckons the deep need for substantial healing of the soul. And until it is discovered that God alone can present the healing balm necessary for our full recovery, these unfortunate souls often evolve into beings that perpetuate the same experience for their progeny—a cycle of fear, anxiety, pain, rejection, depression, isolation, confusion, despondency and despair.

At this stage we have successfully perpetuated the Generational Curse, that spoken of in Exodus 20:5: *"...I, the Lord your God, am a jealous God, visiting the iniquity of the fathers on the children, on the third and fourth generations of those who hate Me, but showing loving-kindness to thousands, to those who love Me and keep My commandments."*

Numbers 14:18 reads in similar fashion:
"The Lord is slow to anger and abundant in loving-kindness, forgiving iniquity and transgression; but He will by no means clear the guilty, visiting the iniquity of the fathers on the children to the third and forth the generations."

I was born-into a severe measure of rejection, and spent my childhood in a deep state of depression, sadness, isolation, loneliness and fear. I would go on to have a life-changing encounter with God in early adulthood (age twenty one). But I did not immediately come to terms with many demonic strongholds in my life—*demons*—which should have been dealt with (i.e., cast-out) upon my conversion and baptism—a practice commonplace within the first century Church, and a practice which has been swept under the carpet through demonic devices (i.e., formalized religion—fueled by the Religious Spirit) at this juncture in Church history. I rather prevented God from doing the deepest figurative heart surgery required for my total healing. Had I learned to better recognize the strongholds in my life early on, I would have known just how to fully embrace Him, and to welcome Him into every chamber of my heart. It would then be many years before I would come to terms with my dire need to allow God to fully inhabit my heart, to then heal so many deep, lingering wounds—and to set to flight the many generational and demonic strongholds in my life.

It was during my non-cooperation with God's plan for my personal healing and deliverance, that I would go on to wound many souls—perpetuating the very brand of pain I met as an infant. Actually, I should be completely honest with you; my personal pain began *in utero—before* I was born.

It would be unfair to characterize the thirty-three years in which I have been involved in the work of the ministry, as that while "wounding many souls." For I have been privileged and honored to have been used in speaking healing to some of the deepest wounds possible, in thousands of lives at this stage in my life. However, I have yet wounded many souls along the way.

It is not my intent to expand upon and fully expose those who inflicted the pain in my early life, as I would be dishonoring them to do so. Much rather, it is my intent in and through this book (which for me is much more of a *personal letter* to you than a book) to be painfully honest about how I allowed my pain to wound others, and more importantly how I then allowed God to absolve me, heal me, and restore me to a place of purpose within His larger plan for my life—a plan which would use the platform of my personal pain to evoke His gracious healing in others.

There is nothing that has happened to us, which was not first *allowed* to happen to us—by God—as the result of the free-agency component of our makeup. Therefore, those who were used as channels of pain toward me as a child were simply pawns, governed often by forces beyond their awareness—forces that were allowed to have their way. True, people had to be willing parties to be used as such, yet I cannot hold them hostage to a spiritual stranglehold through an unforgiving heart—no more than I would wish others to impose a spiritual stranglehold upon *me*, through *their* posture of an unforgiving heart.

We are commanded to honor our fathers and mothers, as Ephesians 6:2 reads: *"Honor your father and mother (which is the first commandment with a promise), that it may be well with you, and that you may live long on the earth"* (Ex 20:12, Deut. 5:16). I therefore presently honor my father and mother, not only as my parents, but as children of God. They have been redeemed, and washed in the blood of the Lamb of God—Y'shua HaMashiach—Jesus the Messiah. I therefore do not hold them accountable for events, which led to my pain and torment, for they simply perpetuated *their* personal pain and torment, long before they met with the saving knowledge of the Messiah. I have sought to underscore this point that the reader would not preclude that I maintain an emotional indictment toward my parents. Much rather, I simply and candidly speak openly about that which contributed to my pain and torment early in life, which by necessity requires that I include my parents in so telling my story.

There are many profound themes within the pages of scripture; the Torah (or Pentateuch), the Tanach (Old Testament), inclusive of the Prophets (Heb., "Neviim)" and Writings (Heb., "Kesuvim") and the B'rit Hadasha (New Testament). Very often, and by divine design, there is a character in scripture that becomes an unusually personal point of identity with each of us. There is something within their story that speaks deeply to our souls; perhaps an uncanny mirror of a portion of our lives. In this context, it is within King David's latter days, as his heart melted under the heat of God's compassion and mercy, as the result of his heart of contrition—as the result of *teshuvah*—a turning away from that which led him astray in his earlier days; which ultimately drove him into the arms of a compassionate, merciful and loving God; that he found healing and restoration.

It is in the context of King David's story therefore, that we find the heart of a man once shattered to pieces in despair, agony and brokenness; to then find his heart melded together by a healing balm as the result of his authentic contrition before God.

As I share my story with you, it is my prayer and petition that some element of such will soften any hard places in your heart—figurative scar tissue as the result of deep heart-wounds, and will enable you to more fully recognize and experience the boundless mercy, compassion, love, healing, deliverance and freedom awaiting you in the arms of God, made possible by the sacrificial Lamb of God—Jesus.

Chapter One

Take Me Up
למעלה אותי קח

One of my earliest childhood memories is that of sitting on the floor, in the corner of a room in a small house in southern California, in my mother's arms, while she wept uncontrollably and sporadically shouted back at my stepfather. There had apparently been a fight of some kind. I don't remember a great deal about my first stepfather. I do recall that he tried to be a father to me. He and my mother divorced sometime not long following the incident that I remember. Following their divorce, he eventually took my younger brother Rob with him, to live in another state. It was before their move out of state, that I recall visiting my stepfather, where Rob was also living, in an apartment in Century City.

I recall my stepfather engaging in practices, which shocked and terrified me. It was while visiting him that my soul felt as if it sought to escape my body, to avoid harm. I recall my insides quivering at what I witnessed. I would later nervously join-in the "fun" in which my stepfather was engaged, along with my younger brother. I've only vague memories of what transpired. The most vivid memory is simply what I felt inside; an attack upon my soul, a bruising of my soul—a bruising, which felt eerily familiar at the time. My stepfather had introduced my younger brother, and ultimately me, to pornography, via a movie projector loaded with such.

As my younger brother later moved to another state with his father, I was too young to define the loss I felt inside. It felt as if a piece of my soul were being torn away. I was still very young, and not old enough to

1

understand and process what was happening.

I vaguely recall a number of family trips to the beaches of southern California with my stepfather, beaches less than an hour from our home at the time. I recall the feeling of breathing-in the majesty of the ocean, the hypnotic cadence of the waves breaking, the wind caressing my ears and the symphony conducted by the seagulls, sandpipers and tiny children squealing as they ran from the incoming water. I would often stand there at the water's edge, looking deep into the horizon, imagining another place and time—wishing I were there.

While still very young, I joined the Nautical Cadet Corps of America—precursory training for the Sea Cadets, which was for teenage boys, age thirteen to seventeen. I knew then, at age ten, that I wanted to travel the oceans one day, on a ship. Subconsciously my quest was that rooted in escaping my current reality, a reality heavily laden with sadness, loneliness and fear. I recall at one point in my Cadet activities, an approaching test on the multitude of knots used aboard a Navy ship. Memorizing them was terrifying, as I was made to feel stupid in elementary school, and feared any kind of test, and I typically rendered poor grades. The knot test was to occur on a weeknight. Just hours before the knot test, consumed in fear, I ran away from home, on my bicycle. I knew only two major roads in our area, and I therefore rode maybe a mile to a large area intersection, and traveled one direction for many miles thereafter. As evening grew, the police managed to track me down and bring me home. I recall my mother holding me tight and weeping, and saying something to the effect that she thought she may have lost me. I later told her I could no longer stay in the Cadet Corps. Without ongoing fatherly reinforcement and coaching, I was simply unable to meet the ongoing study and skill requirements therein. It was a sad departure.

Not long following this period, my mother decided to join a church in a neighboring city. We quickly became good friends with one family in particular, who were prominent leaders in the church. Before too long, and while my younger brother was yet with our family, we were invited to spend the night with this family, we children. The family had a boy who was 2 or 3 years older than me, and a girl who was maybe 4 years older than me. I recall in the middle of the night, awakening to a shocking sensation—the sensation of being sexually molested. In shock, I froze, and did not budge. I was paralyzed with fear. The older boy performing such, moments later briskly returned to his bed when he heard the footsteps of his older sister ascending the steps leading to their rooms which faced each other at the landing of the second floor. His sister momentarily turned the hall light on and peered into his room. This was the second wave of shock and embarrassment that evening. The girl said nothing, and quietly retreated to her room across the landing.

As the day unfolded the following morning, the older boy acted as if nothing had happened, as he appeared convinced that I had been asleep the whole time that he was molesting me. Nor did his sister act as if anything unusual had happened. I did my best to spend the day playing with everyone outside, acting too as if nothing had happened. I recall seeing the family again on several occasions, but I do not recall any subsequent incidents like the first. My mother eventually discontinued attending the church, and throughout my childhood and teen-age years she would not return to a church of any kind. She would never know of the incident. I suspect in retrospect that her instincts prompted her to withdraw from fellowship. The incident vanished from my mind throughout the reminder of my childhood, and would not return to memory until many years later.

This sexual encounter served to further pull me into a predisposition of introversion; into hiding and suppressing my true feelings, and masking them through a personality that was not my true self; a personality that was spawned by fear. This fear would deepen as my elementary school years further unfolded. It was not long before I realized I was hated by the dominant ethnic

3

minority in the area. In truth however, *I* was the ethnic minority. I recall many threats, being pushed and shoved, being spat upon, and knocked to the ground. I was living in the midst of many young gang members, whose older brothers and fathers were violent offenders and longtime gang members. It was the younger fledglings that I had to deal with, for the most part.

I recall on one occasion, peddling my bicycle quickly down a sidewalk, toward a local liquor store to buy candy. I rode around a young gang member walking toward me on the sidewalk at the time. As I passed him, I looked the other way, so as to avoid eye contact, which otherwise seemed to set them off toward me. But the moment I passed him he shoved my handle bars, causing me to flip repeatedly on the concrete. It nearly knocked me unconscious and broke my bicycle frame in at least one place. As I lay there crying, I recall him walking away, turning around with a smile on his face and calling me many vulgar names, using very foul language.

My neighborhood and early school experience was laden with the fear of these kinds of scenarios happening at any moment. I recall on a later occasion peddling my bike on a sidewalk, riding home from a pizza pub, and passing a bus bench where an obvious gang member was seated with his apparent girlfriend. He appeared to be much older than me, by twelve or more years. As I passed the two, I again looked the other way to avoid eye contact. Within a few seconds following, I heard the steady stride of someone chasing me from behind. It was the gang member. He caught-up with me by pulling me off my bike by my hair. As he did so, he began yelling at me with foul language, accusing me of giving his girlfriend a "dirty look." She had then boarded a bus, and as the bus passed he forced me to look up at her by pulling on the hair on the back of my head as the bus passed. With my gaze fixed on the girl on the bus, who was then laughing at me, he punched me in the eye so hard that my head bounced off the sidewalk a fraction of a second later. I then blacked out for a short time, and he disappeared. I recall as I came-to, laying in the gutter, with my bike on top of me, while heavy traffic drove within four feet of my head.

Not long after the beating at the bus stop, perhaps a week later, hiking into the hills above my neighborhood, an area dubbed by the locals "Motorcycle Hill," as older boys and their fathers would often ride dirt bikes therein, in the late afternoons, and throughout weekends. On this day I found an area atop one of the hills that was serene, and with no one in view. I was sitting in the grass with my head in my hands, weeping, with feelings of unspeakable rejection and loneliness. Within a few minutes of sitting there a little mouse popped his head out of a hole of a withered piece of wood lying near me. He did not see me. He was actually looking the opposite direction as he sat up on the edge of his hole. He then began to wash his head, by licking his hands and briskly running his hands across his head. I saw his tiny wet hair poking up as if it had just been shampooed. I realized at that moment, that he too was just as vulnerable as I was, yet somehow he was simply unaffected by the many threats about him. In a strange way, I felt a kinship with this little mouse. My heart melted as I realized how fragile and vulnerable he was—a fragility and vulnerability that I shared. For the moment, I had forgotten my pain, and was solely focused upon his welfare.

To this day, animals have this affect upon me, especially baby animals. Something about their vulnerability, gentleness and fragility makes me melt inside. I cannot recall the thousands of times in my lifetime since, that God has placed a small animal in my path, to melt my heart, and to pull me out of a place of sadness, bitterness and despondency.

Within a year or so after the latest beating, I found myself transferred to a middle school, in the same city. I recall being at a dance, during school hours. I don't recall the specific occasion. I recall approaching a gang member who I thought had become somewhat of a friend to me. He waited until several were in our vicinity, and after looking around to confirm several eyes would witness what would follow, he violently shoved me, so hard that I flew through the air and landed on my back and head. I slowly walked out of the auditorium, found a deserted place near one of the playgrounds, and sat in the grass until it was time to ride a bus home.

I believe it was perhaps just a few days later, over the weekend that I was walking through an alley not far from a new apartment we had moved into; when I suddenly felt a supernatural warmth flood my heart. I also recall feeling the sensation of unusual heat upon my head, as if it were flowing down from my head, and into my heart. I would later understand the feeling to be love—the love of *God*. At that moment I came to a stop, alone in that alley. I then looked up toward the sky, and heard these words: *"I want you to know that I love you, David."* I was stunned, and slowly returned my gaze toward the ground. I recall thinking, *"I am Andy, not David. In any case, it appears that God loves me."* I had been addressed by a nickname within my middle name (Andrew) for all of my childhood.

My memory then drifts to yet another move, a move closer to metropolitan Los Angeles. I recall walking through what I recall to have been Hollenbeck Park, in East Los Angeles. I had my ten-speed bike with me at the time, rolling at my side. I recall being violently shoved into the concrete walk, and my bike being picked up and thrown into the lake at the center of the park. There were maybe five or more gang members around me, who then began to kick and punch me, and then tore off my shirt. After hurling many foul names at me, they eventually left. I managed to retrieve my bike from the water, and found it to be badly damaged, bent in several places. As I returned home that day, I recall returning home with many points of inner turmoil; turmoil over the trauma of what had happened to me less than thirty minutes prior, compounded by the ongoing turmoil of returning to an atmosphere at home that confused me.

One redemptive feature of this home that I recall at the time was that of one very large wall wherein a custom bookcase had been built to accommodate what I recall to be thousands of volumes representing my mother's personal library. As I recall, she was stricken with a severe case of rheumatic fever as a child, and was bedridden for the better part of a year, during which she developed a veracious appetite for reading. Throughout her lifetime she has self-educated to the extent that seeking to quantify her education through commensurate degree programs would leave such programs looking rather scantily clad. I've been blessed by her model, and have subsequently hauled hundreds of pounds of my own books around the country with each move I've made over many years.

My mother later moved us to another city, perhaps not more than thirty minutes from our previous home. Within a short time thereafter I would make some friends who were a little older than I, and who would introduce me to skateboarding and surfing, and ultimately drugs. I recall that we lived roughly forty five minutes from the nearest beach. I began to quickly assimilate into the surf culture, and to experience what it meant to be affirmed by peers, for doing something on a skateboard or a surfboard, which met with their approval. There were many "gutsy" moves within the surf culture, one of which was that of making a "late take-off" on a big wave, just before it broke. This to say that one takes-off when the massive wall of water is vertical, performing a "no-paddle take-off." One then skips down the face, making sporadic contact between the surfboard and the water, nearly free-falling, often followed by a bottom-turn with enough centrifugal force to place the rider horizontal over the water, to then begin working the wave. The late take-off was my signature move, and landed me regular accolades with my new peers. For the first time I experienced what it was to be praised, and accepted (as well as what it was like to be violently slammed onto the ocean floor with brutal force). Whether I pulled-off the late take-off or not, the accolades were the same—it was the daring that was honored. My signature move would later land me on a pile of boulders at the head of a rock jetty, in Seal Beach, wherein witnesses said I must have had "angelic help," to survive.

I had purposefully made an extremely late take-off on a twelve-foot wave, perhaps fifty feet out from the tip of a rock jetty. I lost my footing, bounced down the face of the wave, and was then sucked-up and pitched onto the rocks. My board was demolished, and one of my legs was jammed deep into the rocks. As the incoming water rose over my head I thought it was the end of me. Then mysteriously, my leg pulled free. I must have blacked-out, as moments later I was laying on my back, with a lifeguard leaning over me, who exclaimed, *"Dude, like you must have an angel or something, because you only have a small cut on your foot. You should have been like broken to pieces Dude."*

At this stage, perhaps age thirteen or fourteen; I had experienced several forms of illegal drugs. I had been introduced to drugs in the 7th grade initially, and at this stage was being exposed to a form of PCP known as "angel dust." I was also smoking very potent forms of marijuana and hashish; snorting occasional cocaine, and taking several kinds of barbiturates. This activity too, was a means by which to gain the approval of my peers. Though very insecure and terrified internally, I acted outwardly as if I were enjoying myself while abusing drugs. The affirmation I experienced by these peers served to temporarily fill the deep void of the same.

***

Psalm 27:10

**"My father and my mother have forsaken me,
But the LORD will take me up."**

Reasons are myriad, that we may feel as if our father and mother have forsaken us. For the vast majority of us, our interpretation of having been forsaken is that perception rooted in the confusion wrought of a distorted sense of entitlement. For Western media has largely suggested to most of us, that if our perpetual wants and needs are not met while our parents are with us, we have been forsaken.

For those however, who have truly been forsaken, know that as King David declares "the Lord will take me up," he speaks to that place of intimacy with God which knows His daily nurture, the brand of nurturing that speaks His nearness, His personal affirmation, and His love—toward us.

Just a few verses later (Psalm 27:14), we read:

"Wait for the Lord; be strong, and let your heart take courage; yes, wait for the Lord."

The vast majority of contemporary Christendom has interpreted this verse, specifically the word "wait," to denote the posture of simply being patient; waiting for the Lord to "work things out," while we subdue our internal unrest over the circumstances about us from day to day. Consider however, the possibility that King David was actually referring to the practice and posture of designating portions of every day to simply "wait" – for the Lord's presence—period. Must we wait until we're consumed in anxiety, to glibly restate Psalm 27:14 in our minds, through some soulish effort to convince ourselves that if we quote the verse enough times, He will be faithful to grant us a supernatural measure of *patience*? To the contrary, it is my belief that David knew what it meant to simply still one's self, to sit in prolonged silence, daily, allowing the mind and the emotions to draw back out to sea, leaving the shoreline empty, in such a way that all that can be seen are the graceful and beautiful little Sand Pipers darting about, as they search for sand crabs; a precious sight, if you love animals like I do. It is within the context of this mental picture that I see God honoring our posture of simply waiting before Him—with no agenda, but that to listen to His "still small voice," also rendered "a gentle blowing" in some translations (I Kings 19:12).

It is therefore when we still ourselves, alone, in silence, in solitude, on a daily basis, at a designated time, that we welcome the "still small voice" of God to speak to the deepest core of our being—our very soul. It is in this place, this quiet retreat, daily, early in the morning, or late in the evening, or both ideally, that He then affirms us in ways that mankind cannot. Conversely, it is when we neglect this precious discipline that we succumb to seeking this affirmation from those around us. The latter posture is sadly displayed on any given Saturday or Sunday morning in this country, as many church or synagogue leaders wax eloquent from pulpits, while feasting on the accolades of their adoring fans—seeking to fill the void of affirmation left in their souls as the result of having lost their first love—personal and private intimacy with God.

As we place our fragmented souls, or orphaned souls, before the altar of the Lord, the altar of secret time with Him, He will be faithful to "take us up"; to gather the fragments of our hearts and meld them into a new heart that we may know and feel His very hands affirming our being—taking us up onto His figurative lap. And as we still ourselves long enough to allow Him to do this on a daily basis, we minister to *Him.* Our stillness before Him, our yielding to this lifelong discipline, is ministry far and above anything we can set our hands to within the "work of the ministry" in a public context. Therefore, all that we do as ministering agents thereafter, whether we lead a congregation of ten thousand people, or whether we share the love of God with a perfect stranger in the marketplace; is but secondary to the supreme ministry of stilling ourselves before the Lord in the wee hours of morning, or night—and ministering to Him.

Chapter Two

Pull Me Out
אותי משוך

It was in my early teens, roughly age fourteen, that I experienced my first sexual encounter with the opposite sex. Lynette was perhaps three years older than me, drove a car of her own, and was sexually active. I recall the myriad of emotions running through me with each encounter. I thought I was experiencing what it was like to express love, when in fact I was wholly incapable—I was too damaged to do so. I was yet very sensitive to Lynette, very kind and compassionate, and very grateful for her affection toward me. It seems the relationship continued for nearly a year. I do not recall its end, as my memory is largely damaged and blurred, still. I do remember that Lynette was very loving, and sought to hold me whenever possible. It was the first time in my life that I felt truly wanted. I melted with each embrace.

I recall, as I look back, feeling continual shock and disbelief that Lynette actually wanted to be with me; she actually *loved* me. Though my hormones were running wildly, like most young boys my age at the time, the most meaningful moments with Lynette were those when she was smiling at me, and simply happy to be together with me. The physical intimacy, to the contrary, was nothing more than the product of two wounded souls seeking escape from all that we did not understand nor wish to process. How could we, without a relationship with the Divine?

As time unfolded after my relationship with Lynette, and into my later teen years, there would be other sexual encounters. All of these were superficial, and typical of those who "partied" within my circle of friends. It was therefore common to find one's self in mixed company on a Friday or Saturday night, while all were high on one substance or another, and seeking out a sexual partner to complete the evening. The frail, confused little boy was ever present deep within me, during such frolicking. And because one substance or another intoxicated me, I could rarely recall any substantive bond to speak of, with a girl. I, we, were moving far outside God's orbital design for us. We could not possibly form a bond under such circumstances. Rather, we were simply adding to demonic bondage within ourselves, which would later have to be broken—one soul-tie after another.

I recall at one point during my middle teens; the same time frame in which I was involved with Lynette; my mother introducing me to a friend of hers who happened to be an ex-Marine, and who also happened to be gay. He had learned of my saga of being beaten and bullied, and offered to toughen me up by introducing me to weightlifting, and martial arts. I accepted his offer, and thereafter, for maybe eighteen months or more, I regularly trained with him. I respected him for refraining from indulging his homosexual appetite with me out of respect for my mother. He simply wished to help me, to toughen me up; that he did. For within eighteen months or so, I had packed-on perhaps fifteen pounds of muscle. I had also learned some "close quarters combat" from Frank. It was thereafter that I began to become acquainted with a volcanic measure of anger deep within me—with severe rejection at its core.

I recall on a number of occasions seeking revenge for my earlier beatings. I began to make eye contact when gang members were near. I no longer walked away from, or around them. I rather walked toward them, hoping they would start something. Many times they did, and I finished it. I do not believe my strength and fighting skills made way for me. I rather believe it was the shock I instilled within my would-be tormentors, as I exploded in a violent torrent of fists and feet, not unlike the caricature of the "Tasmanian Devil" cartoon character.

I had avoided traditional sports through my

childhood, as I was skinny and sickly, and was laughed at when sides we being chosen for mandatory games during school. However in my junior year in high school, and that following my intense training with Frank, I had the opportunity for a brief career in football. I was invited to try-out for the JV football team. After the first practice session, the coach invited me to play Nose Tackle, as soon the following week, in a real game. I was shocked at how quickly this came about. I believe I played perhaps 4 games, and was very aggressive, and established myself as the "Tasmanian Devil" in fact, by systematically busting-through the offensive line and attacking the quarter back, often leaving him moaning on the ground. It was during my last game, that I so exploded upon the quarter back that my defensive team captain pulled me aside and reprimanded me for unnecessary roughness. I then exploded on him, and so ended my high school football career.

It was at age 17 that the oldest among the surf-tribe I ran with, chose to join the Navy, to see the world, to surf the world. It was during his brief return home after boot camp that he further fueled the same long-held goal within me. I recall pieces of that summer—the last Summer surfing the beaches of southern California (1977), as if it were yesterday. It was during the evening "glass-off" (a period in the early evenings when winds would die down, and the water would become smooth, "glassy") that I would paddle-out and watch the sunset on the ocean horizon, and while awaiting the sets (series of waves) would fantasize about traveling the world. In reality, the fantasy of traveling the world was more deeply rooted in a desire to escape myself—to escape the terribly hard-hearted young man I had become—who was nothing more than a terrified, broken and fragmented young boy inside.

It was late 1977 that I entered the Navy. Boot Camp presented a very rude awakening to adulthood. I cannot say that it changed me for the better internally, it rather further toughened me up externally, further forging my protective layer of aggression—carefully designed to mask the fear, insecurity and pain which consumed my heart. I recall arm wrestling 106 men in my company during boot camp. I beat them all, and so established myself as a "tough guy." Fear and insecurity will drive a man to fabricate an alter-ego which is very convincing to others— while also terribly damaging to the soul.

At graduation the traditional thing to do was that to invade the nearest "red light district" and do what sailors do. I did. I recall a weekend laden with alcohol and women of the night. I recall feelings of disgust. A part of me sought to convince myself that this is what manhood was about; the conquest of women for the purposes of self-gratification. I also recall however, the unusual sensation of feeling the grief inside these women—a turbulence deep within their souls that *they* were even unaware of. They, like me, masked their pain in a convincing exterior designed to portray someone who was enjoying what they were doing. Internally however, they were lost little girls, with broken and fragmented hearts, just like mine.

It was toward the end of boot camp that the Navy notified me that my "A-School" (specialized training for my chosen naval vocation) had been overbooked when I enlisted. I was then given the option of a release-and-return until the school was available, or a redirection into something different altogether. I was duly sold on an amphibious assault group. The adventurer in me was deeply stirred at this notion. Soon thereafter I found myself experiencing another rude awakening to manhood—manhood, as I then understood it. For the ship upon which I was stationed more resembled a floating prison, with extremely hardened and violent men, who drank like fish and represented a new definition of the phrase: "sexual promiscuity." There were relative few married men on the ship who did not violate their marriage vows while in a foreign port. From a purely humanistic standpoint, months out at sea and the extreme physical, emotional and psychological stressors that such a life comprises, appears to substantiate primate-like behavior of men as they attack the pubs,

15

consume beer, fight among themselves, and frequent women of the night. I therefore became the quintessential sailor; drinking, fighting and chasing women—a womanizer.

While living life on the high seas, traveling to seventeen countries, playing hair-raising war games and engaging in actual espionage two years in a row, I had allowed the works of darkness to forge my soul into a state of deep darkness and emptiness. The ship was infected with pornography. It was not uncommon in the early evenings, to walk through one's compartment (sleeping quarters) and see 90% of the men lying in their "racks" (beds) with a pornographic magazine in their faces.

It was during my 2nd year in the Navy that a strange series of events began to weave themselves around my soul, a series of events, which would later come to represent a recognized tapestry being woven about me, by God Himself.

When I was not piloting small landing craft, in the midst of war games, which at times proved more dangerous than war itself; I was manning the helm of the ship, a 522-foot vessel with perhaps 500 to 700 men aboard, 1/3 of whom were Sailors, the other 2/3's of which were Marines. There were many late nights on the bridge, while behind the helm, and when the deck was silent, with only the listing sound of our wake to be heard. It was then, during these moments that I began to feel the very subtle tug toward a state of being, a mindset, and a heart-posture that was foreign from anything I knew. At first I categorized such as one of the many mystical elements of being out at sea—deep sea— thousands of feet of deep sea. It was not long before I began to wonder if it was God Himself that was doing this strange thing with my heart and mind.

I believe it was during my 2nd major cruise, that I began to sense a subtle despondence toward the typical late nights aboard the ship, wherein my shipmates would end the evening with pot (marijuana), whiskey, pornography and card playing. I found myself often wandering the dark decks, looking out to sea, listening to the hypnotic drone of the engines and smoke stacks, gazing into the unspeakable display of the stars and planets, especially while in the North Atlantic Sea. While also listening to the entrancing cadence of the wake and the waves listing below, I would feel an interior tug to a place that I could only define at the time as that otherworldly. It was then that I began to discover or rather acknowledge a spiritual element of my makeup. My soul was, in so much as I could define such at the time, crying-out for feeding. My carnal being had been fed for many years, with nearly every form of vice known to man. Yet my soul, bruised and battered, and stuffed into a dark, damp corner of my being, had remained lifeless— until now.

It was during one of these rare occasions, when I had some time to linger on the deck of the ship in the evening, alone, that a man named "Russ" appeared next to me. Russ had a glow about his face, a face adorned with a perpetual smile that was genuine. Russ rarely said much; he didn't need to. Russ rather radiated a message, a message of peace and tranquility. He seemed to know my pain, and my hunger for spiritual food. Over a period of several weeks Russ would mysteriously appear next to me when I would find a short window of time in which to linger against a lifeline and stare out to sea. Eventually I asked him the source of his peace and joy. He simply said, "Jesus." During one of the final conversations I can recall with Russ, he said, *"You can welcome Him into your heart, and experience Him just like I have."* Weeks following that conversation I asked hundreds of men if they knew what had happened to Russ, and would describe him to them. None of them could recall ever having met Russ.

Within months of my last encounter with Russ, and following my internal realization that Russ must not have been a product of hallucinogenic drug abuse over several years prior, I found myself amidst another hair-raising military operation in the North Atlantic Sea. It was not uncommon during such naval exercises to work as much as 16 or 18 hours a day, and to get by with as little as 2 to 4 hours of sleep a night. It was during several weeks of such the grueling schedule, and while I was stumbling about in a state of severe fatigue, that I approached the fantail of the ship, and met with a tiny bird sitting on a lifeline. The bird was panting heavily. As I neared the bird I was very surprised that it did not budge. I came to within 2 feet of the bird and realized that it was exhausted. It could not move. It then dawned on me that the bird had likely flown for days, and had now met with the first opportunity to rest. I could see in the bird's eyes, terror, and a desperation which said, *"Please, spare me, I cannot continue, I need rest, please."* I recall melting inside, and discreetly weeping. Once again, a tiny fragile animal had melted my heart. This time however, what gripped me most pointedly was that I saw in this precious bird—*myself.* The bird mirrored precisely what I had become—exhausted by my journey to date, desperate for internal rest, and terribly frightened by the world about me. I named the bird, "Herbie."

It was perhaps the same evening, several hours after my meeting with my birdie friend, that I found myself once again on the dreaded "mid-watch," a nightly watch which spanned midnight to 04:00 a.m. It was roughly 02:00 a.m. that I found myself rotating to aft-lookout, and next to a very large ammo box which must have stood seven feet off the deck, and measured roughly 7 x 7 x 7 feet square. I recall crawling on top of the box, lying down, and becoming awestricken at what I was seeing. As the ship slowly rocked back and forth, millions of stars swept over me, darting back and forth in cadence with the ships movement. Moments later I experienced to date what has become one of the most profound encounters with God of my lifetime. Because the nature of the experience poses a puzzle for most, I will only divulge that He enabled me to briefly experience such a profound measure of His love for me, that I thought I would be consumed in His presence—vaporized by the fiery emotion emanating from His heart.

I suppose the socially acceptable way in which to

categorize this experience is that to label it "an epiphany." In this way it can easily be rationalized as the byproduct of an "overactive imagination."

I recall moments after this encounter with God, several men yelling over my headset, men that had been stationed at other points on the ship during mid-watch, shouting: *"Did you see that?!…What was that that?! Hey, Davenport, did you see that?!"* I couldn't speak. Someone from the bridge was eventually relieved, that they could scurry back to my location to see why I was not responding. I apparently looked shell-shocked, as I was relieved of my duty, and sent to my rack (bed). I was later in the morning awakened by one of my seniors who had discovered that I was overlooked during morning muster on deck. I had slept, as if in a comma, for several hours— right into the first few hours of the workday. I believe to this day that God's grace enabled me to sleep for so long, that I could marinate in the afterglow of His visitation with me.

Later in the day my seniors approached me with concern, as I appeared dazed and disoriented, yet smiling all the while. I was asked if I had been doing drugs. I replied no. They believed me, as I was not associated with the druggies at this stage. Eventually several shipmates who were on the same mid-watch the previous night, approached me about what I saw on the fantail. They each saw a fleeting glimpse of brilliant light over the fantail. All of them concluded it was a "UFO." I simply replied that I never saw it. They all concluded that I was in denial, and they began circulating rumors that I was "probed by a UFO."

As I exited the Navy I did so with remorse; remorse rooted in feeling like a failure, as I had originally purposed to serve 20 years, to earn a commission during the process, and to earn a record to be proud of. As my spiritual metamorphosis had begun however, I found the environment toxic, an environment which sought to keep me within the chains of a very dark and barren existence.

I drove through several states the day after my discharge, to stay with my mother and a new stepfather in the Midwest, in the country, on a small farm. With each mile behind me I meditated upon the violent contrast between the partying I had done in 17 countries, and the bizarre encounters that I had with God toward the end of my enlistment. There was a very real tug-of-war going on in my soul. I felt the game was being played by two beings much larger than I. I drove for 100's of miles in a trance-like state, feeling a deep tug to walk away from a life of despair and vice, and into the arms of the "Jesus" that Russ had told me about.

***

Psalm 31:4, 20

"Thou wilt pull me out of the net which they have secretly laid for me...Thou dost hide them in the secret place of Thy presence from the conspiracies of man; Thou dost keep them secretly in a shelter from the strife of tongues."

It is when we choose to answer the call of God, to respond to His tugging in our hearts, that we can expect a subversive net to be thrown at our feet, a net designed to entrap us and entangle us in the chords of vice, keeping us from redirecting the eternal course of our souls. Whether it be our initial salvation experience, or the call to go yet deeper in our intimacy with Him, we can liken this heart-tug to that of a magnetic pull. However, such the pull is never so great that it violates our freewill. It is therefore the will in mankind, our own volition, which dictates just how many jewels we will find within God's treasure chest of revelation—the ongoing and unfolding revelation of His great love for us.

As I drove for many hours through the country on the way to my temporary home, and with 100s of images behind me from many countries, I began to muse over what I felt on that night, in the middle of the ocean, when God expressed His love to me as I lay on that ammo box. It was on that night, and just prior to the encounter with Him, that I had been feeling suicidal; feeling as if my life would never amount to anything. Despite my encounters with the love of God in "Russ," I was equally visited by terribly dark thoughts. A battle was being waged over me—over my very soul. The reality is that the battle waged over our souls will never cease, until we transition to eternity. However we are promised a "secret place" and a "shelter" in Him, if we will simply chose to remain within His embrace. My soul, at this stage in my life, had been shaped by rejection, violence, shock, depression, fear, anger, loneliness and a terribly distorted understanding of sexuality.

As I continued to drive through beautiful country on my way to my mother's farm in the Midwest, I sought to internally reconcile the emotion I felt with my profound experience with God. To date, the only feelings I had experienced, which came even close to such, was that experienced for just a few moments, during illicit sexual encounters. It was during my encounter with God's love however, that He gave me a nanosecond of what it feels like to be embraced by Him in heaven. It then dawned on me that this is what men like me have sought to find, in and through illicit sex, pornography and lust. It is the vein pursuit to experience the fleeting pleasures of illicit sex, and pornography, which serves a cheap substitute in our deep, guttural quest to water our souls with the love of God. It is this very void which drives men to fall more deeply into such vice.

For the man who has been rejected at birth, or worse, rejected *prior* to birth, in utero; which was that of my personal saga; he remains consumed in a subconscious compulsion to go *back into* the womb, to escape life as he knows it, perhaps to do another "take," to "re-roll the tape"; thus his perpetual preoccupation with the womb—expressed in and through his illicit sexual appetite, lust, and entanglement in pornography. Equally fueling the rejection wound, is that of the insatiable hunger for love. Such the hunger propels the rejection-wound to seek-out any cheap substitute for love—any behavior which will temporarily release the neuro-chemical, *dopamine*—which provides for a fleeting emotional high which feels much like being loved, and being *in*-love. For the dopamine released in a man's brain while viewing sexually explicit images indeed feels very much like love—and like *being* loved—albeit momentarily. These same dynamics can very well apply to a woman who has experienced the same trauma.

Within each of us lies a vast void which can only be filled by God's love. For those who have been deeply wounded as infants, toddlers and children, and more pointedly in and through sexual violation; we find ourselves entrapped in an emotional vortex designed to deceive us into believing that it is also through sex that we will find euphoric release from our pain—albeit but a few seconds worth at a time. King Solomon, in Proverbs 27:20 aptly declared, *"Sheol and Abaddon are never satisfied, nor are the eyes of man ever satisfied."* We are therefore predisposed to search to and fro to feast our eyes upon soulish images, which serve as a cheap substitute for experiencing the love of God.

It has been biologically proven that when we view sexually explicit images, or we mentally rehash illicit sexual experiences, endorphins and dopamine are released into our system, the same endorphins induced by many drugs, resulting in a temporary feeling of euphoria. As we succumb to the perpetual carnal yearning to engage ungodly sex or pornography, we grant continual license to the Accuser of the Brethren, to condemn us, to sentence us to terminal feelings of guilt, condemnation and hopelessness. This is the very "strife of tongues" to which God offers us "shelter," if we will choose to break-free from the chains of bondage herein, by humbling ourselves and crying out to God.

It is then not until we meet with an experience that far outweighs these cheap substitutes, that we remain entrapped by them—entrapped by a "net." Intimacy with God, in and through daily communion with Him, places us in the "shelter" which shields us from the entrapments that are "secretly laid" for us. Until we run into the arms of God, and through the veil of His Son Jesus, we stumble about, entangled in a perpetual net of vice spawned by our wounds—simply fulfilling our job description as carnal beings.

Nestled within the Book of Revelation, and within God's rebuke to the church in Thyatira, we meet with this warning: *"...I have a few things against you, because you allow that woman Jezebel...to teach and seduce My servants to commit sexually immorality...indeed I will cast her into a sickbed, and those who commit adultery with her into great tribulation, unless they repent of their deeds...and all the churches shall know that I am He who searches the minds and hearts"* (Rev., 2:20-23). It is the very spirit of Jezebel that fuels the pornography industry. And for those intoxicated by her lusts, awaits a "sickbed," expressed in two very pointed ways, in my personal experience and observation.

When we engage cyber-sex with a complete stranger, by viewing pornography on the Internet for example, we are damaging our bodies, our temple, just as if we were engaging the *physical* act, whether it be in the form of fornication or adultery. As we do so, we welcome not only demonic habitation, but we also welcome sickness, most pointedly in the form of the loss of life, the shortening of our days, and an acceleration of the aging process. Consider Proverbs 10:27(b), accordingly: *"...the years of the wicked will be shortened."*

John does not expand upon the specific manifestations of Jezebel's "sickbed," however I have personally experienced such judgment, and have also keenly observed the same in the lives of many men, over many years, with whom I have co-labored in the trenches of inner-healing and deliverance, in battling these forces.

Another very pointed manifestation of this sin is the "sickbed" of our finances; a drying-up of financial provision, an all-out assault upon our finances, financial hardship, and perpetual lack therein. Once again, this has been my personal observation and my personal experience in the lives of hundreds if not thousands of others who have battled this specific assault of the spirit of Jezebel. King Solomon in the Book of Proverbs underscores this very dynamic: *"He who covers his sins will not prosper..."* (Prov. 28:13).

The grief I have carried over not only shortening the days of my temple, but also in welcoming financial calamity upon my household, as well as being crippled in my ability to bless those who depend upon me financially, has been often crippling for *me*. It is the cross of Jesus, the blood of Jesus, and the arms of Jesus, which have severed this deeply affixed cord of grief from my heart. It is only in His arms that we find freedom from such hideous entanglement; in *His* arms, versus the arms of a stranger in cyberspace.

Chapter Three

I Kept Silent
שׁוֹתֵק הֶחֱזַקְתִּי

Upon arriving at my mother and stepfather's farm following my discharge from the Navy, it was like taking a step back in time. I recall the feeling of having to tune my right-brain back about 33 megahertz. Having moved more recently from the west coast back to her home state; a return to her extended family in the country; my mother was grateful to be reconnected to family for a time, something she had been completely devoid of for many years while living out west. My stepfather traveled much of the time as an occupation, for him therefore it seemed just another adventure in travel.

My stepfather was the last of a dying breed of men, men raised in the west on horseback; men who had learned to break horses, ride bulls; fell massive redwood trees with 25-pound chainsaws, and hunt big game—all by the age of 13. He was a hulk of a man, one who had served in the Special Forces at one point in time. Though rather late in life for me, I sought for a season to find a father figure in him. I admired the "grit" in him, and his John Wayne-like persona. In some ways I sought to emulate such. Doing so however only served to further mask my brokenness and pain. He would fade from our lives not long thereafter, in the form of another family break-up. He would ultimately give his heart to Jesus, and go on to engage much fruitful ministry abroad.

Within a few weeks of my return home, albeit in the country, on a farm, something far removed from my orbit to date; I found myself quickly matriculating into the party scene of cousins and new friends. My younger sister Amy, not unlike my older sister Kathy, was very attractive, and quite a fixture within the local high school. She in turn attracted a group of young women who would frequent the farm. It was late one evening, when several girls were spending the night with my sister; that one of them, Tina, crawled onto the couch with me as I slept in the living room. As she nestled herself under my blanket, the little boy in me became frightened—as always. My testosterone did a great job however of masking such, by responding in the only way I knew to date, making me just as responsible for our sinful frolic. Nine months later my late night visitor gave birth to a baby girl.

Let's be clear; lest the reader preclude that my mention of Tina crawling onto the couch was that designed to infer that *she* was the perpetrator; I will readily divulge that it could have just as easily been *me* crawling onto the couch—to visit *her*. There, you've been disarmed.

It was during Tina's pregnancy that I became consumed in shock, disbelief and sadness over playing a part in producing a life that to me seemed a terrible mistake at the time. I would thereafter find myself in an all-consuming depression. For I little knew this woman, had no unusual feelings for her, and was certainly wholly unprepared to ponder the notion of marriage. She was certainly likable and loveable, in fact I found her deep-country paradigm of simplicity, enchanting; yet I was simply incapable of relating to her as a boyfriend, let alone a husband.

It was during this dark season, prior to the birth of our daughter Amy, that the Lord began to water the seeds planted in me during my encounter with Him out at sea; through "Russ" aboard the ship; and through the more recent witness from my aunt Linda, and the witness of my uncle Sonny, both of whom lived in the countryside not far from us. During this time I began to wrestle with the notion of moving back west, to stay with my older sister. I had become terrified at the notion of a web having been woven to seal my fate in the country, far removed from anything I aspired to do. My introversion, self-absorption, and fragmented heart would not allow me to even consider sacrificing my life ahead of me, to remain near my daughter, and near her mother. It could have been that God would have interwoven my heart with Tina's. There is no end to what God could have done, had I availed my whole heart to Him at the time. The reality however, was that I was yet wholly self-absorbed, and subsequently incapable of grasping not only Tina's precious worth, but also the precious gift of Amy to both of us. I would later shatter Tina's dreams by moving back west—abandoning she and Amy.

For many years I would harbor disbelief over what had occurred. It would be many years thereafter before I would realize that Tina's heart was just as fragmented as mine, and acting-out primal behavior, in a state of loneliness, fear, and a longing for authentic love and family. It was at this point that I would feel so deeply convicted for holding her in contempt for simply wanting to create a family in the only way she knew how. It would also not be for many years later, that I would realize the impact of my emotions upon our daughter Amy. For it is yet while in the womb, that children absorb the spirits of their parents—emanating love or rejection. Amy therefore, just like me, was born-into a world of rejection.

It would be nearly a decade later that I would meet my daughter Amy, upon my return to the area. She has since grown up to be a strikingly beautiful woman. It was as she was roughly 17 or so, and while she stayed with me for a short time, that I was graced with the opportunity to lead her to Jesus. Many years have passed since that day, all of which have not been without my deep, guttural pain over the years I lost with her, as well as the pain I caused her and her mother, by abandoning them.

***

Psalm 32:3-4

"When I kept silent about my sin, my body wasted away through my groaning all day long. For day and night Thy Hand was heavy upon me; my vitality was drained away as with the fever heat of summer."

It was as I later returned to California with Jesus in my heart, and following my Navy tour and short-lived sojourn in the Midwest, that the Holy Spirit would begin to systematically weave me into the paths of many Believers—my introduction into authentic fellowship of the saints. As I began to nestle-into Church life, the internal struggle to completely die to the old self, and to wholly submit to His interior cleansing became a fierce battle. At the crux of this battle was that of my relative silence about my sin—my sin of abandoning my daughter and her mother.

As we, as Believers, deny the probing hand of the Ruach, the Holy Spirit of God, to fully cleanse our hearts of the old nature, we grant "extended stay" for the demons which would otherwise opt to flee. Denial, dishonesty, pride and self-absorption to the point of narcissism, among many other toxic heart-postures, keeps us in a place of demonic bondage, and will ebb away at the gift of internal peace granted us with new life in Jesus. In His grace, He would during this period yet enable me to experience divine tokens, often in the form of unspeakable joy in His presence, *despite* my hard-heartedness. For I would soon experience the power of His presence in many formal gatherings among Believers. It was when the dust settled following such meetings however, that my "body would waste away" as did King David's, in and through my silence over unresolved sin and corresponding bondage. For God's "hand was heavy upon me" in His dealings with me. And to this day His "hand" remains a growing mystery, in that while He was ushering me into the power of His presence, unveiling many mysteries, He was just as deeply probing my heart—challenging me to "come clean" with all that I sought to hide. And it is not until we "come clean" with Him, and with those we love, that we will ultimately walk in the fullness of that which He has apportioned to us in this lifetime.

To walk in the fullness of all that God has apportioned to us, is to in turn come to know the Father's Heart, to experience His unfathomable love for us; to experience what it means to walk in His authority and anointing; to be used by Him via the temporal mediums of gifts, ministries and ministry offices; and to also experience His loving-kindness. In Psalm 32:10 we read, *"Many are the sorrows of the wicked; but he who trusts in the Lord, loving-kindness shall surround him."*

Trusting in the Lord includes that of responding to the uncomfortable nudging to willingly unveil the deep recesses of our hearts. He has held the pursuit of our *hearts* as His chief goal in this life. He wants our *whole heart,* that He may in turn infuse *His* whole heart—into us. It is as we kick and scream at His probing hand, and we fail to cooperate with His inner-cleansing, that many of the events about us as well as the circumstances in which we find ourselves, are laden with strife, turmoil and anxiety. To the contrary, it is God's intent to surround us with His "loving-kindness," however we cannot recognize such when we purpose to keep Him from cleansing the deepest recesses of our hearts.

His loving-kindness is not always that in the form of an endless supply of peaches-n-cream, but in the form of His peace and grace in the midst of storms which inevitably come our way (i.e., *"In this world you will have tribulation",* John 16:33).

Chapter Four

The Broken Hearted
לב השבור

Just prior to my return to the west coast, I asked Jesus to fully inhabit my heart, following repeated witnessing from my uncle as I stayed with him for a time. His approach was very down-to-earth, very real, very raw; an approach which simply could not be escaped. He did not preach to me, he simply shared from a place of total transparency, readily talking about his weaknesses and struggles, while at the same time acknowledging Jesus' sovereign power to refine Him over time. How can one refute such a raw and real witness? It would be many years later, as a trend visited mainstream Christianity in the form of "WWJD?" bracelets, that I thought back to my uncle Sonny, and answered the question posed in such bracelets: *"What would Jesus do? He would firstly be real."*

To this day I have emulated the model that so impacted me of my uncle Sonny. When I speak abroad, and in the midst of an audience that doesn't know me, I have found that the quickest way to their hearts is that to open my talk with transparency about my failures and struggles. It is truly amazing thereafter, to watch the figurative doors of their hearts swing-open to then receive the fullness of my message. It is in our rawness and realness that the Holy Spirit is granted full liberty to move freely through us, to impact those about us. We rather disrupt His ebb and flow when we allow the toxicity of the Religious Spirit to gum-up the works.

My initial salvation experience with Jesus was truly profound, and ultimately occurred deep in the night, right around 3:33 a.m. I had moved into an apartment in the city not long before returning to California. The apartment buildings in the area were built around the "shotgun" floor plan, so named as one could fire a shotgun into the front door, and expect the buckshot to exit the backdoor—a straight shot from end-to-end. One could also find rapid escape therein, from a would-be father-in-law, wielding the same.

As I tossed and turned late one evening, with the words of my uncle Sonny resounding in my heart, and unable to sleep, I ultimately sat up in bed. Moments following I looked out the window at the foot of my bed, and toward another apartment building directly across the street. It was a narrow street, and the opposing building was maybe 50 feet away. At that moment a light came on in the room directly opposite mine, across the street. I then saw the shadowy movement of several figures moving around in the room. The window was open; it was summertime. I then heard the shadowy figures begin to sing a beautiful song: *"Seek ye first the kingdom of God...and His righteousness...and all these things shall be added unto you...hallelu, hallelu..yah"* (Mathew 6:33). I recall feeling a tugging in my heart which felt like warm hands massaging my heart. At the same time the Holy Spirit was working me over, I recall thinking, *"Are these people completely out of their @*#!&%# minds?! Its 3:30 in the @*!&%# morning!"* The incredible tugging in my heart however quickly overrode my less-than-angelic thoughts at the moment, and at roughly 3:33 a.m. I rolled off my bed and onto the floor, knelt by my bed, and simply prayed: *"Jesus I ask that you would come into my heart, make my heart your home, cleanse me from my wretched state, heal me of my brokenness, and show me how to live."*

After going back to bed, and throughout the remainder of the evening and early morning I would reawaken, sit up in my bed, and feel a tingling sensation in my brain, a sensation which felt as if my brain were being turned—a fraction at a time. As I ultimately fell into a deep sleep thereafter, I would not awaken again until

31

mid-morning, when I would discover that much of the brain damage caused by drug abuse, had been healed. I knew this instantly, as I realized I now looked at the world about me with a clarity I had not experienced before.

It was not long after my conversion, and while working with a Believer, that I would through him be introduced to a woman who struck me as being more angelic than anyone I had ever met. Carole affected me in a way that I had never experienced before. She radiated the love of God, and bore the trademarks of deep intimacy with Him. There was nothing sexual about my attraction to her. Rather, her spiritual beauty mesmerized me. She was outwardly very pretty, but I did not initially see it, as it was so strongly overshadowed by a *spiritual* beauty. For she had spent several years in isolation with Jesus, and had in fact begun the internal process of becoming a nun, dawning a ring on her ring finger which symbolized her marriage to the Lord—and to Him alone.

As my planned departure for the west coast approached, I would enjoy several dates with Carole. For the most part these dates involved fellowship with other Believers, and times in the park jointly pouring over the Bible. I felt as if I were in another world when I was with her, as she would draw God's presence into our time together. I never once recall having carnal thoughts about her, only a pure desire to simply discover what enabled her to so adorn herself in the love and presence of God.

As I departed for the west coast, I purposed to regularly stay in touch with Carole. We exchanged letters for several months, and she ultimately flew out to California for a brief visit. I would later propose to her. I ultimately flew to Kentucky for the wedding ceremony, not long following that we returned to California.

As we began our marriage Carole was aware of my daughter in Kentucky. Amy remained a constant heart-tug for me, an unresolved element deep within my soul, often spawning dreams of holding her, and fathering her, wherein I would later awaken in the night with a deep sadness over losing the early years of her life with her.

Carole meanwhile was so filled with the love of God that being married to her was like being connected intravenously to heavy pain medication. It was yet very early into our marriage that I realized something was terribly wrong. As we approached intimacy she would become deeply upset. Equally so, it was then that I realized something was undone within *me* as well. It would not be until several years later that I would equate my internal feelings of awkwardness, embarrassment, discomfort and shock with the very same feelings I had experienced when I was molested as a child, at roughly age ten. Something deep within me still needed to be healed, and I carried this into our marriage. To further compound matters, Carole had a deep internal commitment to God—and to Him alone. I believe that deep within, she felt violated each time we sought to become intimate. And strangely enough, I too felt violated, as I was *still* a ten-year-old boy on the inside— yet to be healed from the abuse I incurred as a young boy.

Nine months after we were married, to the day, our son David Jr. was born. I will never forget the moment I saw him for the first time. He was such a miracle for me. I simply could not believe that such a broken vessel as I, could have taken part in producing such a precious little being, and completely healthy at that.

Throughout David's infancy I would often take naps on our living room couch, with him lying on my chest, that he could feel my heartbeat. I thought perhaps in doing so it would form a bond between us.

Throughout David's toddlerhood Carole and I would continue to endure a very dysfunctional life of attempted intimacy. It would be late in the evening very often, and as I would drift off to sleep, that I would have recurring dreams of a traumatic experience as a child. And because I did not know then that God often attempts to speak to us in dreams, I completely ignored them. He was attempting to speak to me consistently about a deeply rooted heart-wound within me, a heart-wound which was undermining the ability of Carole and I to truly experience

33

marital intimacy—and a heart-wound which would go on to wound a number of women as the result of my failure to heed God's voice.

Job 33:14-16 reads: *"Indeed, God speaks once or twice, yet no one notices it. In a dream, a vision of the night, when sound sleep falls on men, while they slumber in their beds, then He opens the ears of men, and seals their instruction..."* It would not be until many years thereafter that I would ultimately learn the Holy Spirit's ways and means; His ebb and flow; and the way in which He speaks through His still, small voice, which happens to include that through the medium of *dreams.* I would later discover an often overlooked "thread" throughout scripture wherein many of the pivotal figures in scripture (both Old *and* New Testaments) would be spoken-to in profound measure, in and through dreams. Interestingly, nowhere in scripture do we find any indication of God ceasing to speak to His children in this way.

It was just a few years into our marriage that I would go to work for an armored car division, while also attending an area Bible College in the evenings. It was on the job, during very long hours which often spanned six-day workweeks, that I would again be daily exposed to pornography through my comrades. This re-exposure would further fortify the deep wounds within me; the deep intrusion into my soul; the deep dysfunction within me; and would feed the hungry demons within me who initially gained their stronghold as I was sexually violated as a child.

Though I would do my best to maintain my witness, and would attempt to speak the love of God into many hardened men who were military veterans, retired police officers, and active duty police officers working part-time for the armored car division; the forces of evil would ultimately overwhelm me, so much so that pornography once again became a daily entrée for me, right alongside lunch with "the guys." The subsequent guilt I carried as I returned home each evening was transformed into anger toward Carole. I was terribly abusive toward her, mostly so through disrespect, dominance and insensitivity.

As time marched forward I would go on to experience many power-encounters with God in and through the ministry in which we were involved—despite my demons. It would be on many occasions that the Holy Spirit would arrest me, and break me, whereby I would for a season detach from the dark influences of the work world. It would crush me, to realize how cold and insensitive I could be toward Carole, who was such a godly woman. It would further crush me to realize how I had continually robbed my son of the father he so deserved. He was such a precious little boy, such a precious gift, and I would let him slip through my hands, choosing darkness, numbness, dysfunction, and vice, over the precious gifts of a godly woman and a beautiful son—given to me straight from the Throne Room of grace.

It would not be until many years later that I would discover that I had desperately needed deliverance ministry from the moment I embraced the Lordship of Jesus in the Summer of 1981. I had demonic strongholds in me that needed to be excised. Until I would meet with such deliverance I would go on to deeply wound my wife Carole, and my son, David Jr.

I believe it was when David Jr. was perhaps age five that I ultimately abandoned he and his mother, through separation, and some years later through divorce. Though I saw David weekly, and shared custody of him, I yet deem my actions that of having abandoned him and his mother. Through typical narcissistic rationalization I convinced myself that Carole had driven me from her. I was absorbed in the study of secular psychology at the time in my early post-military college years, and drew upon such to effectively dilute what I knew to be truth in scripture. I recall being mentored by two secular psychology practitioners at the time; one specializing in Cognitive Therapy, the other specializing in Jungian Therapy. Both consistently coddled my demons and almost nearly convinced me that the hybrid nature of my faith (Pentecostal/Charismatic/Evangelical) was a delusion. Such an artful means by which to suppress the truth; it served me well in the short-term, as I began to live a life of wanton compromise thereafter. However, the unspeakable pain and agony of what this did to my heart would eventually catch up with me.

The most miserable human beings on the planet are Christians who artfully hide secret sin over extended periods. For the internal combustion of Holy Spirit-induced conviction and grief, combined with perpetual accusation from the Accuser of the Brethren, leaves one utterly miserable inside, despite the pasted religious church-smile mustered in the presence of others.

For a few years during the time in which Carole and I were separated, I dated other Christian women. In so doing I fell into sexual sin, adultery on my part. Outwardly I had sought to mask my pain by indulging myself. Inwardly however I was in agony. I was attending two very healthy and Holy Spirit-inhabited congregations simultaneously during this period; feeling God's overwhelming presence in worship; while also feeling the unspeakable conviction of grieving the Holy Spirit while living a double-life. Deep in the night the Holy Spirit would prod my soul, alerting me to the depths of sin to which I had fallen.

Ultimately Carole returned to her home state of Kentucky, with David Jr. Their departure was a crushing blow to me. It was as they left that the gravity of my brokenness, dysfunction and hardness settled upon me in full measure. I went into a state of shock, and what one may more precisely describe as *spiritual arrest.*

***

Psalm 34:18

"The Lord is near to the brokenhearted and saves those who are crushed in spirit."

It is very often not until we are brokenhearted and crushed in spirit, having been wounded by another, or in my case brokenhearted over the revelation of the depths of my personal depravity; as well as feeling crushed in spirit by the weight of God's judgment upon me; that the Lord drew near to me as I cried out to Him in despair and agony.

King Solomon stated in Proverbs 29:1, *"A man who hardens his neck after much reproof will suddenly be broken beyond remedy."* I had resisted God's repeated rebuke, and His consistent visitations deep in the night, wherein He was attempting to reveal to me the key to my torment, which kept me bound in the chains of sexual dysfunction, and which kept me hard-hearted to the point of losing this dear woman and my precious son. I had become "broken beyond remedy." Despite my agony and the feeling of being crushed by the weight of God's judgment, He would yet draw near to me each time I cried out to Him.

God's compassion and mercy is unfathomable. Even when we taunt Him and run from Him, and grovel in sin before His omnipresent eyes, and allow our hearts to be figuratively encrusted in stone; He is yet eager to extend His arms to us if we will but fall at His feet, acknowledge our depraved state, become brutally honest with Him and plead with Him for mercy. 1 John 1:9 reads accordingly, *"If we confess our sins, He is faithful and righteous to forgive us our sins and to cleanse us from all unrighteousness."*

It was on the Isle of Patmos, in seclusion, and while likely in a state of loneliness, insecurity, post traumatic shock and depression, that John the Revelator received the most magnificent prophetic vision foretelling the End-Times. Though I cannot know for certain what his countenance was like just prior to the vision, I can read-into the events which led up to his retreat to the island; events which included unrelenting persecution, threats and subsequent hardship of many flavors. Equally so, we can at many points in our lifetimes find ourselves on this figurative Isle of Patmos—exhausted, lonely, confused, and in a state of shellshock following wounds from others, or wounds of our *own making.* And it is precisely at this point that Jesus most typically unveils the greatest depths of His compassion, mercy and forgiveness—as we prostrate ourselves before Him in brokenness and humility.

It is one step further, in verse 19 of Psalm 34; that we read: *"Many are the afflictions of the righteous, but the Lord delivers him out of them all."* Whether our afflictions are that wrought of the works of darkness which violently oppose the callings on our lives, or whether our afflictions are that wrought of the sin which we carefully guard and hide; we have access to the Deliverer, Who is faithful to free us of our chains, if we will simply humble ourselves, and yield ourselves to the deliverance process.

Chapter Five

Resting and Waiting
ומחכה לנוח

It was not long following my relocation and return to the Midwest from the West Coast, and that to live near my son and my daughter; that I would stumble through the doors of an explosive congregation of Believers, which was trademarked at the time as being a truly powerful venue of mercy, compassion, healing and restoration. The presence of the Holy Spirit was so strong in these early meetings that I would weep continuously over my terribly broken state.

I would go on to receive truly life-changing healing of many heart-wounds. I would also go on to serve an internship within this congregation, and subsequently further tap-into my gift-mix and resume various ministries in which I had dabbled on the West Coast, years previous. I would begin to further walk-in various capacities in serving the Body of Christ, and would most pointedly serve as a conduit of mercy, healing and restoration to many broken lives—lives broken like mine. I would begin to travel, and to be used in various conferences, experiencing the electrifying flow of the Holy Spirit moving through me in the revelatory gifts.

It was a truly joyful season in my life, despite the ongoing pain of separation from my son, my daughter, and my former wife. Despite the deep scars upon my heart—scars inflicted by my actions alone, the Lord would see-fit to use me—anyway.

It would be during this season that I would resume seeing my daughter Amy. My heart would melt continually as I would spend time with her. It was truly a miracle for me, that despite my coldness and the fact that I had abandoned her, I was now spending time with her. Only God can weave such a story of restoration.

It would be during this season that I would personally experience the fulfillment of Malachi 4:5-6, which reads:

"Behold I am going to send you Elijah the prophet before the coming of the great and terrible day of the Lord. He will restore the hearts of the fathers to their children and the hearts of the children to their fathers..."

Despite my ongoing pain of separation from my son David Jr. as well, I would also marvel that he still wished to spend time with me. Every time I would see him, I would thank God that despite the terrible pain I had caused him, he would yet be willing to spend time with me.

It was also during this period that I would, through divinely ordered steps, locate my natural Father who I had not seen since my infancy—some thirty-three years previous. Through an initial exchange of letters, we agreed to ultimately meet for a stay in a cabin, in the vicinity of Natural Bridge Kentucky.

The reunion was filled with Holy Spirit power, and the healing of lingering wounds in both of us. My father would shortly thereafter fully embrace the Lordship of Jesus. He presently serves the Body abroad via an Internet ministry that acts as a universal portal for people around the world making online inquiries about life in Christ.

I would later form men's groups, breakfast groups, the foundational teaching of which was that rooted in the miraculous restoration between me and my father—and my son and daughter. I would speak-into many deeply wounded men, who had been torn from their father's through one traumatic event or another. The groups bore much fruit, and many lives were changed as we focused upon heart-issues; the healing of the heart; a focus which, with rare exception, boiled-down to an issue of forgiveness.

It was during this period that I made a concerted effort to avoid relationships with women, which were anything beyond superficial friendships. I simply did not trust my wounded-ness, the lingering numbness, and myself in my heart. Though I met with many points of healing, I yet instinctively felt there was something undone deep within my heart—a numbness which prevented me from loving as I should.

Occasionally through weakness I would allow myself to succumb to a relationship which subtly and gradually became more than mere friendship. When this occurred, I would invariably wound those I dated. I would reach a point of emotional attachment and then abruptly meet with a place in my heart which felt terribly hardened, unfeeling, and barren.

In confusion I would consistently and awkwardly withdraw, leaving women confused, and hurt. There was some mysterious wound deep within my heart, which remained well hidden, yet which began to stir and to surface when feelings and emotions were stirred beyond the norm. It was from this, that I would retreat, and subsequently sever any relationship responsible for stirring or exposing such.

As I retreated and further withdrew from the temptation to date, and to comingle with women, I found myself again spending hours with the Lord, just like the season in which I first met him. It was during this season that He proceeded to purge me, to cleanse me, to break me, to refine me and to humble me—again. It was as I refrained from the urge to pursue a serious relationship with a woman, that He again revealed Himself as my "first love."

I was once again met with the reality of Psalm 37:4, which reads: *"Delight yourself also in the Lord, and He shall give you the desires of your heart."*

It was as I purposed to delight myself in Him and Him alone, that He reassured me that He would give me the desires of my heart—desires which I could not negotiate nor navigate presently, as my heart remained wounded.

As I continued to find myself renewed and daily intimating with the Lord, I felt the deepest caverns of my heart being restored. I yielded myself to several ministry teams offering further inner healing and deliverance. I began to feel a deep heart-purge, and the unveiling and excising of darkness lurking deep in my heart—darkness as the result of festering wounds.

I also recall submitting myself to a few different professional Christian counselors (upon repeated recommendation), who in turn did little more than effectively mask my issues with what I call "candy-coated-Christianity," and who were rather quick to peg me into a given clinical category within the DSM-III-R (Diagnostic and Statistical Manual of Mental Disorders), which in turn laid the groundwork for the suggestion of psychiatric medication—which I simply refused. My "Christian counseling" therefore, did not last very long, thankfully.

It was as I bathed in new life in Christ, that some well-meaning friends of mine, a dear couple, acted upon the fanciful idea of introducing me to a female friend of theirs. Initially I was fearful, as I felt there was more surgery the Lord wished to perform on my heart, before I would have the freedom and liberty to date again. I felt what could only be described as a perpetual twinge of divine jealousy over my soul. I yet succumbed to the temptation to simply know whom it was that my friends wish to introduce me to. I believe it was loneliness that drove me, more than anything else.

Once again, I ignored the still, small voice of the Holy Spirit. I would later realize that He was not seeking to prevent me from meeting this woman; He was rather seeking to prod me to act out of purity, versus brokenness, in relating to any woman.

As I met her, Adrienne, I was immediately captivated by the overwhelming life in her. Several years younger than me, she immediately made me feel as young as she. She shared my passion for music, for creating music, and for worship. She was also beautiful, in every way.

As I began to spend consistent time with her I would continue to feel the Holy Spirit's prodding of my heart to carefully guard my affections, to restrain my emotions, and to simply respect and appreciate Adrienne for who she was—a precious sister in the Lord—not an object into which I might channel my lonely affections.

It was several months into our relationship when late one evening I knelt down at my bedside and asked the Lord, while in prayer, if I would have the liberty to marry her. His response was riveting. His voice was beyond audible, and it permeated my entire being; I felt as if my lungs and heart had stopped functioning for a fraction of a second, when he said simply: "No!"

There have been perhaps a handful of occasions in my life when God has spoken to me in such a way that I have felt physically, psychologically, emotionally, and spiritual paralyzed as the result—this was one of those occasions. And as He rendered His verdict, He also downloaded in perhaps the span of a nanosecond, volumes of information as to why I should not make-motion to marry Adrienne.

In essence and in short, He spoke to me that His wish would be that I learn to love and respect Adrienne as a sister; to learn to love and appreciate her as a friend, and to refrain from allowing my romantic affections to run their course, as in doing so I would nullify a great deal of the healing He had worked in me over a number of years.

Equally, to engage Adrienne romantically, would nullify a great deal of the work of healing He was doing in her. He therefore explained to me, in a fraction of a second, that the finishing touches of my healing, and Adrienne's healing, hinged upon our complete cooperation with Him, which at this juncture meant loving and respecting each other as friends—period. He wished to show she and I what it meant to love and respect someone we were attracted to, all the while refraining from engaging ourselves romantically; a healthy relationship as Believers in Jesus.

In what would be one of the more foolish and terribly destructive decisions of my life, I simply responded: "No, God, I cannot refrain myself from pursuing her. I am terribly lonely, and I love her." What I did not realize as I made this decision, was that God would in turn lift His hand of healing from my life; He would lift His hand of grace over my life, and allow me to walk headlong into my own devices. All that He was working in my heart, through my intimacy with Him, was placed on-hold.

As I continued to pursue Adrienne, wholly ignoring the voice of the Lord, I was released into a delusional state—believing that God would bless our union despite His warning. He had lifted His hand from this union even before it was formed. As He did so, He allowed me to stumble back into the same hard-heartedness and wounded-ness that had destroyed my marriage to Carole.

Almost overnight, literally, and immediately following our wedding, my heart was filled with darkness. I had returned to a heart-posture of selfishness, meanness, callousness and carelessness with Adrienne.

I became a quintessential narcissist. I destroyed our honeymoon, through irritability, anger, and argument. And for several months thereafter I tormented Adrienne through radical mood-swings, callousness, selfishness and angry outbursts.

I had once again fulfilled the sobering promise of Proverbs 29:1: *"A man who hardens his neck after much reproof will suddenly be broken beyond remedy."*

In and through my disobedience to God's voice He released me once again to a state of "brokenness beyond remedy." I began to experience a mental and emotional meltdown.

During such, and on a whim, I made the decision to leave Adrienne, to abandon her, and to stay indefinitely with family in the northwest. I would eventually return to her temporarily, all the while insisting that I was changed.

Nothing in me had changed. I remained under God's severe judgment, and was miserable, equally making Adrienne miserable. I would leave Adrienne once again; this time retreating to family in the southeast, to again stay indefinitely. It would be during this period that I would subject myself to the figurative "backside of the desert," stealing away with the Lord for hours a day, contending for His voice.

It would be during this season that I would feel the full gravity of my sin—my sin of ignoring the unmistakable voice of the Lord. It would also be during this period that a series of prophetic messengers would reveal to me the true depth of my brokenness—the origins of my deepest pain, i.e., sexual molestation as a child, abandonment as a child, severe rejection as a child, and feelings of hopelessness as a child. They shared this with me without knowing anything of me in the natural.

It was these areas specifically that the Lord was healing in me beautifully—before I once again hardened my heart and ignored His voice. In essence, what I had committed was perhaps analogous to that of abruptly removing the hands of a surgeon from his patient in the latter course of open-heart surgery, leaving the patient helpless to the elements.

I would once again submit myself to deliverance ministry during this season, removing the demonic barnacles, which had affixed themselves once again to the walls of my heart. I would later write to Adrienne from the figurative Cave of Adullam, attempting to explain to her a severe season of interior purging—in my figurative desert.

At this stage, I was too late; I had so wounded her that she wanted nothing more to do with me, and deemed me nothing less than a sociopath—and rightfully so. It was hereafter that the gravity of what I had done to her began to fully settle upon me. It was terribly depressing to realize what I had done to her.

Such a precious women, a tremendously gifted woman, with a singing voice which was nothing less than angelic, and a multifaceted artistic ability which was strongly anointed by the Holy Spirit. I had terribly wounded her, and the Holy Spirit enabled me to fully feel her pain. I would for many months melt before the Lord in solitude, weeping over what I had done.

We find a very sobering word nestled deep in the

Torah, the Old Testament, in the form of Deuteronomy 28. Throughout the chapter we are met with a divine dichotomy of the blessings of obedience versus the curses of disobedience.

In the opening verses (vv. 1-2), we read: *"If you diligently obey the voice of the Lord your God...all these blessings shall come upon you, because you obey the voice of the Lord your God."*

Verses 1-14 go on to define more blessings than any one person can contain in a lifetime. Verse 15 however goes on to declare: *"If you do not obey the voice of the Lord your God...;"* and continues on into a hair-raising list of curses through verse 46—more curses than can be endured in a lifetime.

In very simple terms therefore; it is in and through our simple obedience or disobedience to the "voice of the Lord," that we either grant Him liberty to make us whole again, or to return us to a state of fragmentation—as we were when we first fell at His feet as sinners.

He does in fact speak to us, and we can learn to discern His voice, if we will but learn the discipline of stilling ourselves before Him for a period of each day. Discerning His voice however is but half the equation; the other half requires that we obey what we hear.

***

Psalm 37:7:

"Rest in the Lord, and wait patiently for Him..."

Consider what it means, to "rest" in the Lord. The Hebrew word "dä·man'" (דָּמַם), means literally to "be still" and to "be silent." The word denotes that of the posture and practice of ceasing activity—including mental activity—to observe a time of stillness and silence before the Lord—every day. It is as we cultivate this supreme discipline, that we are subsequently graced with a divine level of patience which permeates our being, and which orders our steps.

It was as I rather chose not to "rest" in the knowledge of God's undeniable healing occurring within my heart that I stepped out of His will for my life, and out of His perfect order of restoration. I failed to "wait patiently" for Him.

I subsequently welcomed a hideous curse over my life—again. He removed His hand of healing grace over my life, and allowed the hordes of hell to ravage my mind and emotions, causing me to leave a trail of destruction behind my every step.

Having learned to work on my own automobiles over the years, with the exception of major repairs, and that solely through trial-and-error, with no coaching to speak of; I've often encountered the mis-threading of a nut on a bolt. This to say that the threads within a nut have to perfectly line-up with the threads on a bolt, in order to properly tighten.

If one is not very careful, one can begin a cross-thread process, wherein the nut begins to counter the original thread in a diagonal fashion. When this occurs, the original threads are destroyed, and, very often, the seating (tightening) of the nut and bolt does not occur properly, thus jeopardizing the integrity of the assembly.

To ensure the bolt seats properly on the nut, I often turn the nut in reverse order, which causes it to drop right into place, before then turning it in the standard order—clockwise. So the Holy Spirit often prods us to step-back, in the opposite direction of what we feel we should be headed, that we can be properly "seated," before He resumes threading us into the secure assembly of the next chapter in our lives.

It is as we willfully defy the known will of God that we step out from under the shadow of His wings (Psalm 91) and we exchange such for a dust cloud of demonic oppression, which closely resembles the cloud of dust which permeated the Peanuts cartoon character "Pig-Pen," who, wherever he went, carried with him an aura of dirtiness—a cloud of filth.

Romans 11:22 reads: *"Consider the kindness and severity of God: on those who fell, severity; but toward you, goodness, if you continue in His goodness. Otherwise you also will be cut off."*

I would like to believe that in and through one heart-transaction with Jesus, we can ensure that the eternal state of our soul is locked-into a divine retirement plan. The Word of God however renders a sobering contradiction to such a notion. God's severity is very real, and He deals most severely with those He has called to lead. When the Word says, "you will be cut off," it means precisely that: "you will be cut off."

Matthew 24:13 reads: *"He who endures to the end shall be saved."*

We cannot deny the directness in the Word. The state of our soul eternal is that determined by our willingness to endure to the end. And enduring to the end requires daily sustenance in and through intimacy with Jesus. We find this sustenance as we still ourselves before Him, learn to rest in Him, and subsequently absorb His patience—subsequently trusting that He knows best, for He is intimately acquainted with our deepest yearnings, our deepest pain, our deepest struggles, our strongest temptations, and the frailty of our frames. As we meditate upon King David's many seasons of deep distress throughout the Book of Psalms, we meet with poetic language that erupts from the deepest caverns of his heart.

In Psalm 42:7 we read: *"Deep calls unto deep at the noise of your waterfalls; all your waves and billows have gone over me."*

It is when we purpose to still ourselves before Him, knowing full well that as we do so we give Him license to probe the depths of our hearts; that the depths of the Holy Spirit's probing and healing calls out to the depths of our brokenness. As we then yield ourselves fully to his painful probing, we fully relinquish the totality of our being—releasing our rights, submitting to Him as a bond slave. And it is as we die to the carnal agenda within each of us, which runs radically contrary to the Holy Spirit's ways and means, that God's purposes will overwhelm us, not unlike massive waves consuming us and thrusting us to the ocean floor.

As one who surfed for 3 decades, and often in large, violent surf, I've an uncanny understanding of what it feels like for God's "waves" and "billows" to envelope a soul. I've been slammed on the ocean floor so violently that I've nearly been knocked unconscious.

I had entered into such a season with Him—again, a season characterized by my willingness once again to figuratively lie upon an operating table, with my hands strapped to my sides—wholly yielded to His scalpel—very much aware of the agonizing pain that awaited me.

Chapter Six

A New Song
חדש שיר

    In the first chapter of the Book of Galatians (vv. 11-18) we meet with a passage which contains a very potent revelation, and which is all too often glossed-over, even by very seasoned students of scripture. As we *meditate* on scripture however, versus that of *studying* scripture, we will meet with underlying treasures of revelation—treasures that *transform*. In this context, consider the Apostle Paul's reflection of his initial calling to preach the gospel: *"...the gospel which was preached by me is not according to man. For I neither received it from man, nor was I taught it, but I received it through a revelation of Jesus Christ...I did not immediately consult with flesh and blood, nor did I go up to Jerusalem to those who were apostles before me; but I went to* <u>Arabia</u>*...three years later I went up to Jerusalem..."*

    In essence, and in very simple terms, Paul received a personal revelation of Jesus Christ—a personal *encounter* with Him; after which he did not in turn seek to be mentored, shepherded, interned, schooled, trained and ordained by the hands of men. What did he rather do? He went to the *desert*—the desert of Arabia—where he learned to daily commune in intimacy with the Lord. Then, *"three years later"* he *"went up to Jerusalem,"* thereafter engaging one of many powerful chapters of his ministry.

    It is in this figurative "Arabia," or "the backside of the desert," that we encounter God in far more profound ways than that rather orchestrated by the hands of men. In the desert there is little food, little water, little shelter, little comfort and convenience. Rather there is little more than you—*and God.*

Surly, there is merit in submitting to the tutelage of seasoned veterans who have gone before, however such tutelage pales in comparison to what occurs within our hearts and souls when we purposefully retreat into solitude with the Lover of our souls—Jesus—for an extended season. And it was *my* figurative "Arabia" which I stumbled into, as I found myself on the heels of having nearly destroyed the life of yet *another* precious woman of God, through my extreme brokenness and the demonic strongholds which had once again been allowed to encrust and encase my heart; that I once again met with the mercy of God.

To date countless leaders; mature, seasoned, gifted and anointed leaders had poured-into my life over a period of many years. I yet failed to allow the Holy Spirit to so permeate my spiritual fiber that I would forever be yielded and melded to His ways and means—for eternity. This permeation can *only* occur in "Arabia," in the barren place, in the desolate place, in the backside of the desert, where all that is heard is the listing of the still, small voice of the Lord Himself. It is in and through these encounters, in this place, these seasons; that the chaff of our lives is burned away by a Refiner's fire, revealing deeper layers of Christ-likeness in our souls and countenance thereafter.

Once again, and during this season of retreat, I submitted myself to the hands of a deliverance ministry team, who drove-out the demonic strongholds in my life. I was again freed from the demonic chains upon my mind and emotions. It was during this period that I began to better understand what is categorized as a Generational Curse—a force that overrides our best intentions, and that not unlike a tsunami, which overpowers and devastates everything in its path. It would be during this season in the desert that I would once again greet a series of generational forces warring against my life. This would result in multiple renunciations of such demonic forces. I do not share these dynamics to in turn suggest that I was not personally responsible for the work of my hands in wounding others, for it was my will that *chose* to cave-in to such forces. I rather explain this dynamic to in turn explain how it was that I would once again yield to the dictates of darkness, which would so deeply wound another Believer.

Again I found myself spending hours pouring-over scripture, sitting in stillness and in silence, fasting regularly, and denying myself the luxury of socializing. During this period I also began to pray that God would place figurative blinders around my eyes, not unlike those worn by race horses; blinders that would prevent my eyes from unduly registering upon a woman. He began to answer this prayer, and in supernatural fashion I would find myself in large congregational meetings, and my eyes would simply not register the presence of a woman as they had before. I subsequently became solely focused upon what *God* was doing in a given meeting. My carnal senses were in the "OFF" position, as an answer to prayer. This would go on for several years.

Though it is understandable that the collective voice of secular psychology would deem my pseudo-celibate state to be unhealthy, I yet benefitted tremendously by removing myself from socialization, and rather focusing solely upon the meditation of scripture, and daily periods of lingering in God's presence for hours at a time.

It was during this extended season of renewed spiritual consummation with the Lord, that a steady stream of revelation began to flow through my heart. This was not the kind of revelation I was seeking at the time. To the contrary, this steady stream was that comprised of brief segments of anguish experienced by those that I had so deeply wounded in my lifetime. Beginning with Tina; then Amy, then Carole, then David Jr., and ultimately Adrienne; I experienced the very anguish that each of them had felt, having been traumatized by me—by my unhealed wounds. The Holy Spirit knew how crippling it would be for me to feel the full-weight of the pain I had caused so many, over so many years. He therefore

imparted it to me in survivable doses. He did not engage
me in this way to torment me; much rather I would later
understand such to be that of the very *answer to my
prayers*—prayers that begged Him to so crucify my carnal
nature that I would never again be capable of wounding
another human being in the ways that I had. Part of this
crucifixion entailed the systematic experience of
empathetically experiencing elements of the anguish I had
caused. It devastated me.

Living in a rural setting at the time, there was little
room for social distraction after my work hours. I would
then typically retreat to an apartment within a very rustic
and quaint 150-year-old schoolhouse, in a very small
town. My floors were littered with books—my only friends
at this stage in my life. I would meditate upon 100s of
biographies of spiritual forerunners who had strongly
impacted the Body of Christ abroad during their lifetimes.
In so doing I would discover two prominent threads
within the tapestries of their stories. The first of these
threads was represented by a lifetime of *suffering*, and
that very often in the form of physical maladies. The
second prominent thread in the lives of so many history-
makers, was that of *persecution*—predominantly so in the
form of those *within* the walls of the *Church* at large—
persecution far in excess of those without the walls—the
"heathen." It became increasingly clearer to me that to
offer one's self as a bond-slave in the service of the Lord,
was to relinquish our perceived rights, and our sense of
entitlement to personal happiness in this lifetime—
personal happiness defined by those things which feed
the needs and wants which Western society has so
successfully suggested we must have, even as Believers.

It became increasingly clearer during this return to
the "backside of the desert—Arabia," that I was once
again being stripped of the mental and emotional
confusion wrought of my deepest wounds—those wounds
which lurked deep within the caverns of my heart. It was
during this desert-season that I began to wonder if I
would best serve humanity for the remainder of my days
by finding the supernatural wherewithal to hereafter live

a celibate life, and to die completely to the yearning for female companionship. I convinced myself that this was my lot.

In time I found the courage to re-assimilate into Church life, by attending a large congregation not too far from my rural hermitage. The congregation was alive with a season of powerful visitation, a dynamic trademarked by the sporadic outpouring of powerful measures of the Holy Spirit's presence. As a rule, I remained toward the rearmost rows in the very large sanctuary, and also sought to come and go in ways wherein I was largely unseen. I sought not to gravitate toward resuming the reigns of the work of the ministry, but to rather sit, soak and saturate in the presence of the Lord.

Perhaps nine months would go by, and through my interaction with many within the congregation it was discovered that I played guitar, and that I had led worship previously, among other things. I was then asked to join the worship team. Though it was exhilarating to again find myself within the organism of a truly gifted and anointed worship team, and to once again experience the dynamics of the Holy Spirit hovering upon a platform during such; I was yet not completely comfortable in front of such a large sea of people. As an introvert I continued to remain fearful in the face of large numbers of people. I would defuse this ongoing fear by focusing upon a portion of the ceiling toward the back of the large sanctuary. I found that by doing so I would not only free myself of the fear of so many onlookers, I would also, by default, become more so focused upon God's presence, while also remaining free of the carnal temptation to perform for the masses—versus truly worshiping the Lord.

It was during one such worship experience within a large and electrifying gathering one evening, that I removed my gaze from the ceiling of the back of the sanctuary, and looked down upon a woman making her way through the sea of people near the platform. I recall feeling at the moment, that what I was doing was autonomic, and perhaps more so *Spirit*-guided than anything else. I recall feeling the familiar internal dynamics of dawning prophetic lenses, and the feeling that I would briefly glimpse something of a prophetic nature. As I briefly fixed my gaze upon this woman, I immediately saw-into her heart. As I did, my heart melted at what I saw. In but a fraction of a second, I saw that she had weathered pain, loss and sorrow unspeakable in her lifetime. I also saw that she harbored a deep and unwavering love and devotion to the Lord. Moments later as she vanished from the crowd, I felt what can only be described as the Holy Spirit's nudging and prodding to get to know this woman—wholly removed from any natural dynamics in this regard.

As weeks unfolded following this experience, I engaged a deeply tumultuous wrestling match internally. I would see this woman from afar, and while yet feeling the unmistakable prodding of the Holy Spirit to talk to her, I would also feel the unmistakable fear of deeply wounding another woman. Though I had received deep inner healing and cleansing of very deeply-seated wounds once again, I yet feared that I would facilitate a repeat of history.

Over many weeks I ultimately concluded that the steady prodding to meet this woman, after several years in seclusion, was a *divine* prodding, and that again wholly removed from any carnal yearning. In time I worked-up the nerve to introduce myself to the woman I would come to know as Gigi. Within a short period she would agree to visit an area forest preserve with me, to spend an afternoon hiking in the woods. It was during this hike that I began to feel an usual bond with her, a bond which seems to this day to have been forged long before we met. For within minutes we both had found the grace to speak directly from the heart, bypassing any measure of superficiality.

Gigi would later accept my marriage proposal, and we would go on to experience a wedding ceremony which was truly otherworldly in its devotion to the Lord. We would also spend our honeymoon in a desolate area of the Outer Banks of North Carolina, on the beach, at Cape Hatteras, home of the infamous spiral lighthouse. It would be that during the initial weeks and months of our union I would discover the depths of spiritual maturity in Gigi, and the subsequent beauty she radiated as the result. It became clear very quickly that soon she and I would be co-laboring in the work of the ministry, and partnering in such a way as if we had been partners for a very long time. This was an unusually sobering experience, as we both concluded that God had paired us up not for our personal happiness, but for His Kingdom purposes in ministering to the most broken people on the planet—those who had been ravaged like us; those who had also trudged through the mire and muck of figurative trench warfare, and who had emerged traumatized and badly wounded.

Within a matter of but a few months we found ourselves co-laboring in the shepherding of many people through multiple home meetings we facilitated, as well as meetings within the larger congregation in which we were attached. We labored alongside each other very naturally, and we worked in such a way as if we had done so for many years previous.

It is a marvel and a mystery, that the Holy Spirit weaves Himself into the fabric of a union; a union comprised of two broken, torn, traumatized and crushed souls; and graces them with an anointing to speak-into the depths of others. Demonstrated in both of our lives, was the beauty of His marvelous work of restoration.

Gigi had lost her mother while she was yet a teen; had been traumatized in her first marriage as the result of ongoing adultery committed by her spouse at the time; had lost her precious daughter of ten years of age to heart disease; and was watching her father die of advanced stages of lung cancer as we dated. He passed away shortly after we were married. Gigi had therefore equally trudged through the trenches of deep suffering and loss, for much of her life to date. In and through such her soul had been forged into one exuding wisdom, compassion, love, grace and an unwavering devotion to life in the Word. She had poured-over scripture for many years, and the major tenets of such were deeply rooted in her heart.

It became increasingly clear as we continued to minister together that Gigi represented a formidable force against the works of darkness, as she was so strongly rooted and grounded in the Word of God, and also through her daily intimacy with the Lord. I marvel today, some fifteen years later, that God has granted me such a gift as she.

I realize that the notion of divorce and remarriage outside of what scripture defines as acceptable, is cause for great contention. To dispel the potential for the same within the recounting of my story, I'll simply say that scripture is quite clear on the matter. In fact, I insert a timely maxim from one of my favorite theologians at this juncture: *"If the plain sense* [of scripture] *makes sense, seek no other sense, or you may very well wind up with nonsense."* And the plain sense of scripture suggests that Gigi and I committed adultery as we married. Did we knowingly defile the dictates of scripture? No, we did not; it was the furthest thing from our minds. Does the fact that it was "the furthest thing from our minds" exclude us from God's judgment in this regard? No, it does not. Does God forgive adultery? Yes, He does, when the sinner is wholly contrite before Him, broken, and acknowledging the full-weight of his sin. *"How could you David, after so many years of God's severe dealings with you, once again commit adultery, by re-marrying?"* I've no answer for you, other than to say I'm guilty.

Why, the reader may ask, have I introduced this ill-timed theological vignette into the doctrinal foray of divorce and remarriage? I'm glad you asked, dear reader. The effectiveness and fruitfulness of the unusual brand of ministry in which I daily engage is viciously countered ongoing by those moving in a spirit of *Legalism,* fueled by a dragon of a spirit known as the *Religious Spirit.* As such, I often meet with red-faced, bloodshot-eyed, angry theological antagonists who feel it their only mission in life to thoroughly discredit everything I set my hands to within the work of the ministry. I therefore disarm them, and leave them figuratively toothless, when I offer to them that I am in fact the *worst of sinners*, and guilty of every conceivable sin they can possibly think of. Once I've established that, and have also confessed my ongoing secret sin of cat-juggling (i.e., juggling small kittens as if they were tennis balls), they are quickly dumbfounded and retreat, with their tails between their legs (*Note: By the way; just kidding about the cat juggling. I am a passionate animal-lover and I am honored to presently host three kitty-meisters in or about my house).

And, when my dear antagonists are *really* persistent, I remind them that Jesus Himself said those who incubate mental motion pictures of adultery in their *hearts* have committed it as if they had equally done it with their *bodies* (Matt. 5:27-28). I thereafter invite those who've yet to commit adultery in their *hearts*—to cast the first stone at me.

Despite my sin, Gigi remains a gift to me. And He has seen-fit to use the both of us fruitfully so for 15 years at this juncture in time. Our marriage has not been without struggles and trials. Equally it has afforded us glimpses of the divine, the unmistakable presence of God moving through us on thousands of occasions as we embrace the most broken people on the planet. He has redeemed us and used us as a team—despite our equally broken pasts. For this, we praise Him and thank Him daily.

***

Psalm 40:1-3

"I waited patiently for the Lord; and He inclined to me and heard my cry. He brought me up out of the pit of destruction, out of the miry clay, and set my feet upon a rock, making my footsteps firm. He put a new song in my mouth..."

Exploring the varied Hebrew names of God makes for a very rich study. For example: El Elyon (The Most High God), El Shaddai (The Lord Almighty), El Olam (The Everlasting God), Jehovah Shamma (The Lord is There), Jehovah Mekoddishkem (The Lord Who Sanctifies You), etc. All of God's names as we know them reveal marvelous facets of His omniscience and omnipotence. Our God is a God of many things. Meditating upon each known name is not unlike looking through a kaleidoscope, whereby the colors and shapes are ever changing.

One of the greatest contemporary Bible teachers living, whose teaching I was privileged to personally sit-under for a sporadic nine-year period (a man in a place of apostolic leadership and international influence at the time of this writing); while teaching from the Book of Revelation; once quipped: *"I have often pondered how the angelic host around the Throne Room can remain content to simply say, 'holy, holy, holy'—repeating the same word over and over again."* Within the congregation on this day, sat a Messianic Jewish Believer who (in addition to other figurative "treasure hunts" in which he had engaged over many years) had spent many years sifting through the treasure of the Hebrew language. Uncharacteristic of the protocol for the congregation during this Sunday morning message; as the meetings were then, and still are, televised; the visiting Messianic Believer raised his hand and said: *"I believe, sir, that I may have an answer for you."* Somewhat startled by the notion of someone speaking-out during a televised service, and that within a massive congregation, the teacher, being ever-sensitive to the ebb-and-flow of the Holy Spirit, knew instinctively that this was a divine moment, and replied, *"Dear friend, do share with us what is on your mind."*

The Messianic Jewish brother, in a reserved, shy and under-spoken tone, replied, *"It is my belief that as they gaze upon the Lamb of God, His radiance and countenance; His beauty, changes not unlike the hues generated from a precious diamond as it is slowly turned in the sunshine. Moment by moment the angels therefore see a different facet of His holiness, and cannot help but react by again exclaiming, 'holy, holy, holy is the Lord Most High'."*

I do not believe I was in attendance during this particular meeting. I do not doubt however that the Holy Spirit then draped the entire meeting in His presence thereafter. A well-known Messianic singer/songwriter, musician and worship leader would go on to write a majestic song entitled, *The Diamond Turns*, a song based upon the revelation of this humble Messianic Jew.

As I ponder the many names of God, paramount among all of His known attributes to me, is that of how He has revealed Himself to me personally as *Jehovah Rapha—The Lord That Heals—The God of Restoration*.

For many of us, our lives at various stages have resembled the aftermath of a vehicle blown-up by a terrorist's bomb—a blackened, charred, twisted, fragmented smoking heap of destruction. For many of us as well, the "IED" (Incendiary Explosive Device) responsible for the blast is that of an overwhelming tidal wave in the form of a Generational Curse over our lives—a force released *before* we were born. Many of us never see it coming; it simply devastates everything in its path— with little warning. For others of us, the "IED" is that of our own making; the result of our repeated defiance of a Holy God who requires holiness of *us*. For yet others; the "IED" represents a two-fold composition of both a generational curse *and* our failure to heed the visible tentacles of such, by dabbling in "the sins of our fathers" (Exodus 34:7) in wanton fashion.

When alluding to the dynamic of generational curses and sins, I have often used an analogy of someone hearing a knock on their door. They look through the peephole and see that it is an unwanted guest. At this moment, they can make a choice as to whether or not they will open the door. The Holy Spirit very often acts as the "peep-hole," allowing us to gain a glimpse of the visitor who has "come knocking." Those who have cultivated keen spiritual sensitivity (discernment) will back-away from the door, preventing the visitor from gaining entrance. Those who rather *open* the door in ignorance however, often meet with the "IED," and shortly thereafter resemble the wreckage described above.

Irrespective of how terribly fragmented our lives may become; the Lord will in fact hear our cry as we would opt to approach Him with brokenness and contrition. Thereafter He can very well lift us up and out of the pit of destruction, and place a "new song" in our mouths.

It is timely to consider that the vast majority of the heart-wrenching and truly passionate worship songs composed by King David were not simply that of his spontaneous resolve (e.g., *"Say, I think I'll write another song about the Lord and see how it fares in the market"),* but rather that as the result of the painstaking determination to pry himself off the floor and command his hand to express the combination of shock, terror, joy and gladness within his experiences with the multifaceted majesty of God. Much of the same was penned in the face of God's merciful redemption following David's grueling aftermath of carnage which he had personally created.

I am reminded of something the late Richard Wurmbrand (a Messianic Jewish pastor) shared in his book, *In God's Underground.* Wurmbrand spent fourteen years between the 1950's and 1960's, in communist-ran prisons in Romania, being repeatedly tortured for his refusal to cease functioning as a leader within the underground Church. Enduring unspeakable torture, Wurmbrand observed the unfolding of a marvelous mystery. When he would gravitate toward someone whose countenance was consumed in the presence of the Holy Spirit, evidenced by love, grace and compassion on their lips despite the living hell of their surrounds; he would prod them to tell their story. With few exceptions, those who exuded and radiated the most profound levels of God's presence in and on their lives were those who had been the greatest sinners before their imprisonment. The depths of their depravity prior to imprisonment had in turn led them to prostrate themselves before the Lord in agonizing remorse; and once He showered them with all-consuming mercy, they would go on to dig a commensurate well of intimacy with Him as the result. These men whose lives had met with the "IED" of circumstances, as the result of their utter depravity, had received a commensurate level of God's compassion— wholly countering their sins (including murder, adultery, sexual perversion, theft, etc,). Wurmbrand found therefore, that the greatest sinners very often became the greatest *saints* when placed within the Refiner's Fire of suffering. Be encouraged therefore, dear reader, if you have fallen prey to believing that you are beyond redemption.

King David fell to the greatest depths of depravity in and through his personal sin. However as the result of his heart of contrition, he met with the Lord's unfathomable compassion. Subsequently, David lived, moved and breathed God's compassion toward others thereafter, and sang of such most beautifully, for the remainder of his days. This, dear reader, is the "new song" which David sang in Psalm 40. This is also the "new song" which God will give *you*, as you purpose to cultivate and carefully guard your heart of contrition before Him—as He begins to restore the charred fragments of your life.

Chapter Seven

He Knows
יודע הוא

The topic of Deliverance Ministry is typically one which immediately creates stomach acid in most people, for two reasons chiefly: 1) It has been wrought with terrible blunders, excesses and abuses over many decades within contemporary church history; and 2) Many who hear the phrase or topic in conversation—often need deliverance *themselves*—and begin to noticeably squirm.

Within a few weeks (at the time of this writing) I will celebrate 33 years of life in Christ. Of those 33 years, maybe 20 were spent in relative alignment with what God wished me to be doing at the time. The other 13 or so were spent running from His deeper and more substantive purposes in my life, and/or defying His grace by engaging in secret sin in one form or another. And within this 33-year span, the Holy Spirit has artfully coached me into seasons of recognized and affirmed gifts and offices in ministry. In walking-out such I have found that He very often changes the landscape of our "personal ministry vision," and uses us in capacities which are new, and different, to include higher levels of authority, anointing, influence, etc. Often times this occurs when we least expect it, and when we feel least prepared or qualified. One such season in this regard has been that which entails facilitating Deliverance Ministry, which is a relatively recent season. Though I have engaged this facet of ministry sporadically, over many years, it was not until the past two years that I have availed myself to engaging such on a weekly basis. I will share with embarrassing honesty that I *ran* from the inner-tug to facilitate this facet of ministry, for many years. For it was almost daily that Proverbs 24:11 would be supernaturally placed before me:

"Deliver those who are being taken away to death, and those who are staggering to slaughter, oh hold them back."

At the same time the Holy Spirit would place this verse before me, He would also speak to me that it was precisely because *I* had been nearly "taken away to death" on many occasions by the works of darkness, and was also "staggering to slaughter" under the same influences over many years; that I was well-groomed for such the ministry. He had given me authority in the very areas where I was once utterly consumed by demonic strongholds.

It was as I ultimately yielded to a season of facilitating such ministry for those suffering that was I able to in turn draw upon all that I had seen modeled in such ministry over many years, while personally seeking deliverance. It was as I reflected upon the many teams that I had submitted to over many years, that I realized how varied and seemingly at-odds the many methodologies and ministry models were—elements of all of which were fruitful to one degree or another. I began to realize over time that no one deliverance model was more effective than another; just different. I also began to realize that no one deliverance ministry session was the same. The varied methodologies and models point to many points of contrast and even contradiction. The reality is that the essence of deliverance ministry is quite simple; it involves firstly, walking in authority—by *knowing* our authority. One of the more commonly quoted excerpts of scripture in this regard, is that of Luke 10:19, which reads:

"I have given you power and authority to tread on serpents and scorpions, and over all the power of the enemy, and nothing will injure you."

While we have been given this authority, our adversary the Devil has *also* been given "power and authority" in areas of our lives where we welcome works of darkness—knowingly or *unknowingly*. Two of the more frequent "welcome mats" for the works of darkness in our lives are those of Un-forgiveness and Denial. As well, these often co-labor in tandem with one another. The remedy for both is actually quite simple: *forgive*, and be *truthful* about yourself—it's really *that* simple. These two points of volition, if acted upon daily, would revolutionize the lives of millions if not *billions*, immediately.

Those who move in strong prophetic roles within the Body of Christ for example, are especially prone to masking the truth about themselves, as the result of deep rejection. The rejection-wounds spawn a very subtle yet very present underlying fear that much of what they utter will be rejected. They subsequently fall-prey to the embellishment of their spiritual experiences so as to win the attention and acceptance of Believers at large. The perpetual distortion of our experiences with God may impress many others for a while, but it does not impress the Lord. The same Hand that imparted His anointing upon a life can just as easily take it away. And when we are truthful about ourselves, in every way, it releases Him to weave a tapestry of grace around all of our dealings, enabling others to see *Jesus* on the inside—irrespective of the absence of the spiritual platitudes contained in our hyper-prophetic experiences.

Non-Believers on the other hand, do what non-Believers are *supposed to do*—that of stumbling about in spiritual darkness, often destroying themselves, and others, as they stumble. It is therefore rather easy to forgive them as they stumble over us, for they know no better. It is quite different however when a Believer in *Jesus* wounds us, for they're supposed to *know better*. The deepest demonic roots that I have observed are those rooted in bitterness toward other Believers. Very often the subjects were once very close and very trusting of one another, only to meet with a deathly dagger of slander for example at a most unsuspecting moment in time. The reality is that Satan's hordes strategize to turn Believers against one another, thus creating a "house divided." This is a master-strategy of his. Very often the Gift of Discernment will unveil this scheme to us, freeing us from the temptation to take protracted offense. Equally often however, we fall-prey to such schemes, and find ourselves within the epicenter of relational carnage. It is as we draw ever closer in intimacy with Jesus, that we are able to rise above the offenses, for it is in this place of dwelling in His presence that we are often granted a glimpse of *His* perspective, that we might therefore see why people wound us as they do, and can thereafter with grace, opt to love them anyway. Knowing where to get our affirmation has *everything* to do with our ability to remain free of offenses. Our affirmation is found within the arms of Jesus, within His embrace, and during time with Him— alone.

It was very early on in my deliverance ministry experience that a mentor underscored the profound yet very practical "ministry model" which Jesus Himself employed, in John chapter 5. In verse 19 we read: *"...the Son can do nothing Himself, unless it is something He sees the Father doing..."* And in verse 30 we read, *"...I can do nothing of My Own initiative, as I hear, I judge..."* In practical terms therefore, Jesus continually prayed for the eyes-to-see and the ears-to-hear what the Father was doing and saying from moment to moment. As we pray this daily therefore, we are privy to what the Father is doing and saying about the life of another, and we may therefore more easily see them through *His* lenses, and again find it easier to overlook an offense. Hearing His heartbeat above and beyond the noise and chatter of hurtful words, requires daily leaning against His chest, in the posture depicted in Mathew 18:3, i.e., *"like a little child."* As we then figuratively make time to sit on His lap, receiving His embrace, we hear His heartbeat for ourselves—*and* His Heartbeat for *others*. Thereafter, wherever we go, and in whatever we're doing, we hear His heartbeat. And as we simply speak His heartbeat, we are moving in the highest level of revelation as we share the love of God with a love-starved human race.

The same applies to deliverance ministry, whereas very often we can be shown precisely what He is doing and saying to the heart of another, often times contrary to what they themselves are seeing and hearing and verbalizing to be their "issues." It is as this occurs, that a heart of love, compassion, mercy and forgiveness is critical, for these components comprise the Father's Heart for those in bondage; those who are staggering toward the slaughter.

The Holy Spirit whispered to me repeatedly, over many years, that the fullness of my authority, anointing and fruitfulness in Him, while engaging the work of the ministry abroad, would be that rooted in the commensurate level to which I would be willing to be transparent, vulnerable and brutally honest before people, about my past. It was because of this very pointed and personal requirement that I ran for many years from much of what He was calling me to do with respect to speaking-into the Bride, the Church at large. It was not until I began to become brutally honest from the pulpit that I began to experience the fullness of His power as I would speak and minister before the masses.

I have observed four general categories of honesty in which most people operate: 1) politically correct honesty; 2) socially acceptable honesty; 3) mildly discomforting honesty; and 4) *brutal* honesty. I believe it is the latter that we are called-to in this hour, especially that while behind the pulpit.

With so many ministry-models for deliverance ministry in circulation, and with so many abuses and excesses, it is understandable that much of the mainstream Church shy's away from such ministry. Many ministries have made deliverance into a complex science, which suggests a person cannot be delivered unless they enroll in a particular program and obtain a certificate of some sort. The reality remains however, that in very simple terms, *authority* and *truth* are all that are required to send demons back to the pit where they belong. The varied methodologies very often muddy the water.

Demons and/or devils are addressed in over 70 places within the pages of scripture. In the B'rit Hadasha or New Testament, Jesus' methodology for driving them out was a simple two-step process: 1) *"shut up!"* and 2) *"come out!"* The reality however in the contemporary/westernized Church, is that we taboo and/or ignore such ministry. As the result, the vast majority of Believers in our midst are in fact demonically oppressed to varying degrees. In Jesus' day (and the days have become *much darker* since then) the casting-out of demon's was "all in a day's work." I do believe therefore that one of the prominent trademarks of the mature Church as we march further into the End-Times; and as we further rediscover our authority in this regard; will be that of very active Deliverance Ministry in our midst.

One of the prominent characteristics of the truly beautiful chapters of contemporary church history reflected in the Argentinian Revival which has spanned over four decades at this stage, is that of the overwhelming numbers of people daily delivered of demonic oppression and strongholds. Having read several books written by the primary players involved in this revival, I have marveled at the repeated emphasis upon the reality that the vast majority of those experiencing deliverance in these meetings, are "church people." In corresponding fashion, the same players who have ventured to speak and minister at conferences in the U.S. over many years, have collectively observed the Church at large in the U.S. to be overwhelmingly infested with demonic strongholds, represented by tens of millions of Believers wholly unaware of their dire need to be rid of demons—largely because the topic is tabooed from the pulpit, and deliverance ministry as a whole is equally tabooed. One of the reasons is that rooted in an erroneous notion that "a Christian cannot have a demon." Let's be very simple here; the issue is that rooted in how we define the word "have." For there is a very sharp distinction between being oppressed and being possessed. Christians in the West are largely oppressed, en masse.

As I have occasion to speak to large numbers of

people within a given ministry venue, and that while on the topic of deliverance ministry, I make it a point to share a very practical analogy of the dynamics of a car wash. When we drive up to an automatic car wash we are typically given three price options. Option 1 is a "Quick Rinse." Option 2 is an "Economy Wash & Rinse." Option 3 however includes under-carriage wash; tire gloss, spotless rinse and wax. I apply these car wash options to deliverance ministry, and I encourage all Believers to annually consider submitting themselves to a deliverance team, and in so doing to select "Option 3." With the level of darkness presently swooning about us from moment to moment, especially here within the demonic-media-saturated West, it is extremely difficult to remain free of demonic influence and habitation. In humility therefore, we must seriously consider submitting ourselves ongoing to the deliverance process, to remain free of defilement. I recommend an "annual checkup" in this regard.

Many of those in *authentic* (key word) leadership especially, have at one season or another in their lives submitted to deliverance ministry. However, over time the reality of Mathew 12:43-45 has played itself out in their lives:

"When the unclean spirit goes out of a man it passes through waterless places seeking rest, and does not find it. Then it says, 'I will return to my house from which I came'; and when it comes, it finds it unoccupied, swept, and put in order. Then it goes along and takes with it seven other spirits more wicked than itself, and they go in and live there; and the last state of that man becomes worse than the first. That is the way it will also be with this evil generation."

What, let us ask ourselves, does Jesus mean when He describes a house *"unoccupied, swept, and put in order"*? And why would such a condition of a house enable demons to *reoccupy*? Perhaps what Jesus was getting at, is that the house should be <u>occupied</u>—by the *fullness of His indwelling—the fullness of His indwelling within every room, every hallway, and every closet in our hearts.*

The above analogy also bears unilateral depiction of much of mainstream denominational Christianity in the West, presently. For very often, a given meeting place is swept, put in order, is squeaky-clean, and facilitated with great precision. However, the Holy Spirit is rarely to be found, as the atmosphere is alarmingly sterile—a telltale sign of a venue inhabited by the Religious Spirit. Accordingly, Proverbs 14:4 contains a critical message for the Bride of Christ, with respect to facilitating the ebb-n-flow of the Holy Spirit in our midst as we gather. Proverbs 14:4 reads, *"Where no oxen are, the manger is clean. But much increase comes by the strength of the ox."* As applied to Church life therefore, when we allow the Holy Spirit to have His way in our midst as we gather, the "ox" (those actually carrying-out the hands-on work of the ministry, representing also the collective "strength" of all present) will get messy at times, as we release people to do the work of the ministry. But it is in and through the messes subsequently created as the result, that we experience the "increase"—the fruits of the Holy Spirit moving freely in our midst. As we therefore suppress the potential for a "mess" by preventing the Holy Spirit of having His way in our midst, and we sterilize the venue with religiosity, we can rest assured that He will honor such the posture, and opt to spend His time elsewhere.

It was during my first mission to Israel that I was eventually graced with the opportunity to pray at the Western Wall, the Kotel. At the time, and following a lengthy and sporadic fast, my spiritual sensitivities where heightened. My "spiritual antennae" were in the fully extracted position therefore, and I could sense a unique measure and form of God's presence emanating from the Wall. With each step I took, and as I came closer, the Holy Spirit magnified a verse that I should pray. The verse is Ezekiel 36:26:

"I will give you a new heart, and put a new spirit within you; and I will remove the heart of stone from your flesh

and give you a heart of flesh."

I recall placing my hands against the wall, breathing deeply and slowly; I tilted my head back slightly, and began praying this verse. I simply said, *"Lord, please soften the hard places, the scars, the places where I am numb; bring sensitivity back to those places. Further heal those places."* I immediately felt His power surging through my heart in circular fashion, as if it were coming from the wall, into me through my left hand, up my arm, through my heart, out through my right arm, and back out into the wall through my right hand. Wholly unexpectedly (isn't this the way "Jehovah-Sneaky" often works?), each time His power flushed through my heart, I was made aware of deep recesses in my heart where I had closed Him out, subsequently *en*closing things that continued to keep me in places of bondage. Each time I was shown these places, He would ask me: *"Do you want Me there?"* I would then reply, *"Yes."*

This went on for a good fifteen minutes or so, at which point my physiological construct was on system-overload, and I had to back away from the wall. I was feeling overwhelmed at this point. As I was regaining my composure I had a funny fleeting flash of a thought, wherein I pictured my clothes in a heap, smoldering at the base of the wall—with my body nowhere in sight, as I had been vaporized. Moments later I regrouped with a dear friend who was watching me from a distance. He simply said, *"Are you alright David?"* I simply shook my head and said, *"Not really, but that's a good thing."*

Among other things that occurred to me as I processed this experience at the Wall for the remainder of the day, was that of the timely reminder that it is the condition of our *hearts* that is of supreme importance to God. He is not so much interested in what we are doing with our hands, as what we are doing with our *hearts*. When our *heart* is in-order, our *hands* come into alignment.

Twenty-one days prior to my first pilgrimage to Israel I began a fast that would last through my departure. It was perhaps seven days into the fast that the Holy Spirit began pointedly preparing me for my time at the Western Wall, by placing His finger upon areas of my heart that required further purging. One area in particular was that within a deep recess of my heart; a well-hidden corridor that was harboring unauthorized affections. I gave this to Him, and allowed Him to purge me thoroughly. It would be not long following this purging that I would detect a pattern within the hearts of many that I would counsel through deliverance ministry, who would harbor the same. This turn-about thoroughly underscored the dynamics of our earned spiritual authority as the result of healing and deliverance from the same affliction or bondage that we thereafter minister *to*, in others. For as we overcome strongholds in our own lives, we are granted authority to help others overcome the same.

Deliverance ministry however is not just about being freed from demonic strongholds in our lives; it is more pointedly about freeing every cavern within the deep recesses over our *hearts*, which then enables the Holy Spirit to have full occupancy therein. It is not until we purpose to carefully attend to our hearts ongoing, and in this way, that we will experience the fullness of His manifest presence not only *in* our hearts, but *through* our hearts as we minister to others.

Almost by the *minute* at this stage, and that via mass-media-manipulation, we can view an advertisement on television, the Internet, or on the radio, which is much of a flash-in-the-pan presentation resulting in an immediate audio-visual captivation of our senses. Within moments something is often very compellingly introduced. Interestingly however, the closing seconds of a given advertisement often entails extremely fine print (television and Internet), or extremely accelerated language (radio). The extremely fine print and the extremely accelerated language comprise the *disclaimer*, which in essence says, *"None of what you have just seen and heard is true. We are pulling something over on you. We've just conveyed half-truths, and what you really get if you buy-into our pitch, is far removed from what we've just promised."* I use this telling analogy to alight upon many of the more prominent voices in high-exposure ministry presently here in the West, who are gracing the airwaves and thousands of book covers and web pages. From the same, we very often meet with a compelling word therein; but something is *missing.* Our discernment tells us that what is being conveyed is not fully assimilating and watering our soul like it should. This is because a disclaimer has been dully attached to the word, not unlike the hyper-speed babbling voice that follows radio advertisements. For while these personalities often share what seems a compelling word, it cannot be fully ingested within the listener as the babbling chatter of the disclaimer is overriding it. The disclaimer in this context, is that of the hidden places deep within the recesses of the hearts of these personalities, which prevent these vessels from fully yielding to the Holy Spirit's habitation, thus preventing Him from gracing the same with anointing and authority—anointing and authority which arrests the hearts of those listening to, or reading, what should otherwise be a word-in-season.

As we quickly race further into End-Times events, those who daily *practice His presence* will more readily discern the wheat from the chaff of what is being spoon-fed to the Western church. For those who are to the contrary caught-up and into the fear and anxiety-laden events appearing on the TV screen by the minute; the tendency will be that to fall-prey to the attractive option of the drive-through theological espresso available around every corner, and which stimulates for a short span, yet then does nothing more than prevent you from sleeping through the night—in the end.

1 Peter 1:1-2 contains the following salutation: *"To those...who are chosen according to the foreknowledge of God the Father, by the sanctifying work of the Spirit, to obey Jesus Christ and be sprinkled by His blood..."* The Greek word (*agiazo*) rendered "sanctification" in English, means among other things, *"to purify internally, by renewing the soul."* I tend to believe the sanctification

process is that *ongoing*; of course beginning initially as we embrace Jesus as Lord. The Religious Spirit would rather have us believe that we can "arrive" at a place of sanctification—and remain there, as if to suggest we've reached a place of immunity from defilement hereafter. This notion is reflected in much writing, speaking and teaching within many mainstream denominations in this country. Unfortunately this doctrine has missed the mark. The "mark" (bull's eye) happens to be pointedly reflected in "the back of the Book," by way of Revelation 22:14, which reads:

"Blessed are those who wash their robes, so that they may have the right to the tree of life, and may enter by the gates into the city."

Note that the context herein is that of an *ongoing act*, versus a one-time transaction. In essence, the Christian saga can be summed-up in this one verse, which denotes the daily washing of our robes (the daily sanctification of our souls).

Until we learn to "wash our robes" on a daily basis, we will continue to succumb to entrapments which subtly weave their webs deep within the recesses of our hearts, and prevent the Holy Spirit from fully having His way with, in, and through our vessel. One such entrapment is the self-delusion of concluding that we have reached a place of sanctification (i.e., immunity) which places us above defilement. We wash our robes as we spend time daily at the feet of Jesus, being *real* with Him. As we grow accustomed to being real with Him, we also grow accustomed to being real with the *masses*—even when we face a sea of such from a privileged pulpit.

Time with Him, lying figuratively naked before Him, allows Him to purge our hearts from ongoing defilement. When we neglect this critical romance with Him, confusion sets in. On this note, I do believe the following analogy to be rather timely.

A few months ago my wife and I were driving home and were passing a farm (that's pretty much *all* you pass in our neck of the woods) when we noticed a tiny creature on the side of the road just a few inches from 60 mile per hour traffic. We recognized it as a tiny kitten. We pulled into the next driveway, attached to a very large farm. As we made our way back to the roadside to retrieve the kitten, we could see that it was terribly sick; and not more than 4 1/2 or 5 weeks old. It was suffering from severe malnutrition, was dehydrated, covered in cow manure; its eyes were encrusted with infection; and running such a high fever that it was wholly clueless to the danger of vehicles whizzing-by just inches from its little nose. I had never before seen such a sick kitten. I'm confident it would have been dead that evening, either through sickness or being run over by a car, had we not rescued it. Having owned many animals, including farm animals, and having rescued many as well, we've become spontaneous in doing such a thing without a second thought.

In the case of this desperate kitten, our hearts melted at the sight of such a precious creature only inches and moments away from death. We have since nurtured the little guy ("Wylie") back to health, through much prayer and multiple antibiotics. Within the first few weeks of his recovery however, and as is customary with the many profound things we learn from our animals; we noticed that as we placed food before him, while also petting him, he would toggle between devouring the food that his body so desperately needed, and running into our arms to receive desperately needed affection, consolation and security. Even as he was starving, little Wylie would take a slurp of milk in one moment, and immediately turn into our arms to receive a stroke in the next, to then run back to his milk-dish, and repeat this pattern until the milk or food was finished. He was both starved for physical food *and* emotional food, and could not decide which one he wanted most.

So it is with us, in that as we neglect the open-arms of Jesus via precious time with Him on a daily basis, we run toward what *appears* to be the food we need to survive (i.e., the smorgasbord of preaching, teaching, ministry, etc., which is being heaped before us at every turn in the road), when it is the food of His *loving embrace* which will sustain our souls—far beyond the "food" being offered to us by anyone else. Jesus said to His disciples in John 4:32: *"I have food to eat that you do not know about."* It is *this* food which sustains us far more than anything that man can serve us.

When we draw near to Him, and stay there, He systematically speaks to us, very often in subtle, gentle ways, about the condition of our hearts—every room, every cavern, every corridor. And it is in this place of intimacy that we remain free of demonic infestation. Evil influences rage about us perpetually in this age, and they will only increase in intensity as the End Times further unfold. But one seemingly insignificant act of compromise can welcome demonic torment. We stay above such tactics by remaining figuratively naked before Jesus, confessing everything that wars against what we *know* to be contrary to His will for our lives.

***

Psalm 44:21(b)

"...He knows the secret of the heart."

This side of heaven we may never fully understand the depths of God's mercy, grace and love for us. That He knows the secrets within our hearts, and yet chooses to love us unconditionally, should be depth *enough.* It is yet difficult for us to grasp His love for us as the Accuser of the Brethren is presently doing an artful job of condemning us day and night for each and every sin and failure strewn about our trails behind us, appearing not unlike debris which collects on either side of alleyways in dreary industrialized areas of the inner city.

I have found a key in silencing the Accuser however; it is that of *worship.* When we worship the Lamb of God, the Accuser flees. When we worship, we draw near to God, and He promises that as we draw *near to*

Him, He will draw near to us (James 4:8). The dynamics of drawing near to God can be likened to moving a candle in the direction of a pesky fly—it flees, as it cannot continue to buzz about in the face of the flame. So it is that as we draw near to God in worship, the demons of accusation cannot remain on our shoulders, and must flee.

Worship will be at the epicenter of our job descriptions in heaven. This life therefore, is one protracted opportunity in which to practice, and to prepare. Why does worship move the heart of God? It moves His heart because it requires unique sacrifice on our part, to worship Him in purity of heart—to *truly* worship Him. For this requires our determination to exalt Him, despite the anguish, depression, bitterness, fear, anxiety and confusion which so commonly consumes us. When we choose to break-out of our often narcissistic orbits (especially here in the West) and we determine to rather exalt Him, to praise Him, to worship Him with abandon, we are in effect saying to Him that He is greater than all that plagues us. Worship is to *spiritual* warfare what a nuclear bomb is to *conventional* warfare—it vaporizes everything in its wake. Worship therefore, *is* our warfare.

The primary characteristic of the Bride of Christ as She draws ever closer to Her wedding day, will be that of worship taking center-stage in our gatherings. God inhabits the praises of His people, and if we therefore wish Him to fully inhabit our gatherings, we must keep worship at the epicenter of all that we do, and that with increased focus as the End Times further unfold before us.

The Psalm 33:3 calling is going-out to the highways and byways around the globe presently: *"Sing to Him a new song; play skillfully with a shout of joy."* This "new song" is very often a spontaneous outbreak that launches from the platform of an otherwise commonly known worship tune. This *new song* will be fresh and alive with a prophetic declaration, and it will be laced with power, authority and anointing to heal and to deliver—*on the spot.* Instantaneous healing and deliverance will soon become commonplace during our worship services. Many of us have received tokens of such over many years, as God has drawn near and manifested Himself in unique and protracted ways, over many distinctly different seasons within contemporary church history. But this time, it will be very different—His presence will be such that knees will become weak—our knees will naturally be inclined to buckle, as we bow before the approaching Lamb—an unmistakable sign of His drawing near.

Over the past year alone, I have interacted with 100's people in their 60's, 70's and beyond, who have experienced the collective nudging to pick up a musical instrument again, when they had laid such down decades previous. In many cases the instrument was never learned, as it was nothing more than a protracted fancy, never acted upon. But now, so many years later, an unexplainable nudge persists, and the irrational thought of learning the instrument "so late in life" is prevalent; it just won't go away. For some, their instrument is their *voice*, and they find themselves singing and worshipping more so than usual. These dynamics again speak to me of the nearness of Jesus' return. And as He returns, He will be at the spearhead of the *restoration of all things*—which includes the restoration of your heart, dear reader.

Chapter Eight

He Shall Hear
ישמע הוא

We have taken an unexpected turn in our meditation upon *teshuvah,* and my story herein, as we have found ourselves meditating upon the dynamics of worship—of all things. We will soon see however that worship was at the epicenter of King David's restoration following his exposed fall with Bathsheba.

Thus far in my story I have systematically alluded to many excerpts of the Psalms, excerpts which speak deeply of the human saga. And as we continue to meditate upon the Psalms, and the very heart of David, we arrive at the most critical turning-point of David's life—Chapter 51, wherein the entire chapter is laden with David's unspeakable anguish, turmoil and brokenness over the conviction of His sin. The weight of such is almost too much for him to bear, as He fully realizes that it is against God *Himself* that he has sinned.

The progression of David's anguish, grief and brokenness fully mirrors the same pattern that we exude as we experience the full weight of Holy Spirit conviction. For it is typically in the place of quiet retrospect, and after the dust and debris has settled following our personal sin, that we begin to realize that foremost we have sinned against *God*—far beyond our sin against ourselves and others. As David weeps over what he has done, and he experiences the full weight of God's conviction, his weeping begins to serve as a cleansing stream, a stream that leads him to the feet of HaShem. And it is at the feet of Jesus that he begins to worship Him from the deepest depths of his heart. And so it is that in the deepest place of our personal brokenness we discover the only way

out—which is *up*, and "up" is that in the form of our
worship and adoration of the God of Restoration.
Understand that as God restores, He restores our purpose
and alignment with His *will*, foremost. For when God
restores He does far more than simply take us back to
place prior to our loss and destruction; it is not a matter
of going back; much rather it is that of moving *forward*—
and into the unfolding of His perfect will and purpose for
our lives.

The prophet Jeremiah, in Lamentations 3:22-23
declared, *"...His compassions fail not, they are new every
morning. Great is Your faithfulness."* It was in kind that
each morning after David's moment-of-truth with the
prophet Nathan; and not unlike the dew which appears
on the grass each morning; that David met with a new
measure of God's compassion, grace, mercy and
restoration.

In Psalm 51:1-2, David declared: *"Have mercy upon
me O God, according to Your loving-kindness; according to
the multitude of your tender mercies, blot out my
transgressions. Wash me thoroughly from my iniquity, and
cleanse me from my sin."* In like manner, it was God's
word to an unfaithful Israel, through the prophet Isaiah,
that underscored the reality that He could in fact "blot
out" the record of sin: *"I, even I, am the one Who wipes out
your transgressions for My own sake, and I will not
remember your sins"* (Isaiah 43:25).

It is extremely difficult for us; and that irrespective
of our level of spiritual maturity; to accept that God can
completely forget our sins—completely blotting them out.
By scriptural contrast; and perhaps one example through
which we are led to believe that our sins are on
permanent record, is that wherein we are told that every
careless word we speak in this lifetime will be a careless
word that we will have to account for, in the hereafter
(Matt. 12:36). This apparent contradiction in scripture is
the result of our failure to rather consider the *whole
counsel* of scripture (i.e., *"the sum of Your Word is truth,"*
Ps. 119:160). For scripture equally declares, that as
"...we confess our sins to Him, He is faithful and just to

forgive us our sins" (1 John 1:9). He forgives, however our Accuser does not. And it is the *Accuser* therefore that we must silence. We do so most effectively by *worshipping* the Lamb of God.

The fiery trials and pressures of this life are surly enough to negotiate within the context of a given day. When we then heap mounds of unresolved heart-issues on top of this we become veritable pressure-cookers, doomed to overheat, bubble-up and ruin what is otherwise "cooking."

Ovens, and bread *baking* in ovens, often appear in dreams. Very often the prophetic symbolism is that of spiritual *food* being prepared (baked) within our hearts, in preparation for serving such to others; that is, a confirmation of the work of the ministry flowing fruitfully through our lives—or, that which is *about* to. When our hearts rather become filled with unresolved guilt and anguish, we spoil the loaf being baked within the oven of our hearts—a loaf otherwise symbolizing a "word in season" for those around us. Accepting therefore, that we are truly forgiven of our sins as we lay prostrate before God in contrition, is vital to our forward-motion in walking-out all that He has called us to in this lifetime.

In Psalm 51:6, David declares, *"You desire truth in the inward parts, and in the hidden part you will make me to know wisdom."* It is as we are first truthful with *ourselves*, that we are in turn freed to be truthful before *God*. As we are then truthful before God, we are freed to be boldly truthful with those around us. It is in and through our fear and insecurity of being found out, that we feed the strongholds guilt, self-accusation and ultimately self-hatred (in many cases). For if we listen to the Accuser long enough, he will convince us that our sins warrant perpetual self-condemnation, leaving us to feel that we must mask the striped prison uniforms of our convict status, with a superficial charade designed to convince others of our hyper-spirituality. It is very often that those who are perpetually preoccupied with touting their ministerial exploits are *also* those who happen to have yet come to terms with "truth in the inward parts."

As David's *Psalm of Repentance* progresses through Chapter 51, we arrive at verse 10, and a critical pivot-point in His petition before God:

"Create in me a clean heart, O God, and renew a steadfast spirit within me."

At this stage David has given God license to conduct the heart surgery that David knows he desperately needs. David has been granted understanding of what it means to progress with the cleansing of his heart, for he knows that to have a clean heart is to be blessed with a *steadfast spirit*—the opposite of instability and insecurity. As our hearts are cleansed we are granted a steadfast spirit, a spirit with focus, and a spirit freed of the tethers of unresolved guilt.

Within ancient Hebrew culture, as well as that preserved present day through rabbinic oral tradition; the heart was the cradle of the will, the mind, and the emotions. One's understanding therefore was commonly understood to be rather reflective of their *heart*, versus their mind. The Jewish-ness of Jesus is so reflected in His ongoing retorts to the Pharisees and Sadducees of His day, as we read for example in Matthew 9:4: *"Why are you thinking evil in your hearts?"* Thinking, in the heart? This opposes Western rationale, and it is Western rationale that is largely responsible for the demons of Doctrine and Theology which have so infected and infested the Western Church, subsequently excising the Gospel from our *hearts* and reseating it neatly and carefully within our *minds*—in the form of acceptable Doctrine and Theology. To be sure, sound doctrine and theology serve as the plumb line of our faith, however we in the West have created idols of such, so much so that very often where doctrine and theology are heralded as the preeminent goal, the Holy Spirit is *nowhere to be found.*

It is as we further transition to verse 12 of Psalm Chapter 51, that David pleads with God to restore to him *"the joy of Your Salvation."* It is as we continue to reconcile with God the deepest stains within our hearts,

83

that the joy of His salvation is preserved, and renewed, not unlike a tree receiving a refreshing rain. As we mature in the Lord we often fall prey to the subtle compulsion to posture our maturity, reflected in and through the careful resistance to the inner nudging to periodically let our hair down and talk openly of our struggles. For many of us, it is the fear of religious reprisal that keeps us bound. And this fear is substantiated, as I have personally been deeply wounded by those who've listened to my transparency, only to respond with a dagger of religiosity, spiritual platitudes, and judgment. The reality however is that we are called to remain "as little children" (Matthew 18:3) in our dialogue with God, and with others, in the form of purity and trust. Those who subsequently respond with toxic religiosity and judgment have perpetuated pitfalls for *themselves*. Our response is that to remain free of the residue of ungodly judgment, and to remain rooted in the brand of affirmation that only *God* can give, as we continue to intimate with Him on a daily basis. For it is as we neglect our daily intimacy with Him, thus forfeiting His personal affirmation in our lives, that we resort to seeking it from others, whereupon when we are erroneously judged, we are devastated emotionally. Where, therefore, are your getting your affirmation presently?

Verse17 of Psalm 51 approaches the very epicenter of the reason that I have composed this book, dear reader. And it is as we carefully meditate upon verse 17, that I ask you to open your heart to receive the full weight of David's exclamation herein:

*"The sacrifices of God are a broken spirit; **a broken and a contrite heart**, O God, You will not despise."*

Herein is "David's Key"—His **heart of contrition**. Sincere penitence and remorse for our carnal state is the "key" that David found as he bathed himself in rivers of tears, all the while listening to the writhing of his stomach as he fasted in God's presence. Equally, a "broken" heart is one broken of pride, arrogance, haughtiness and self-assurance; it is a heart wholly dependent upon God's grace, God's provision, and God's affirmation.

It was this very state to which the Apostle Paul had evolved as he addressed the Church in Galatia, as reflected in Galatians 4:13-14: *"...you know that it was because of a bodily illness that I preached the gospel to you for the first time; and that which was a trial to you in my bodily condition you did not despise nor loathe...".* Paul suffered severe persecution, imprisonment, hunger, and homelessness; was beaten and stoned, and often appeared as a vagabond; sick from extreme exposure to the elements and lack of nutrition. His suffering rendered him devoid of haughtiness, and graced him with humility—and "a broken and contrite heart." It was manna from heaven that sustained Paul—far beyond earthly food. And it was the same manna that King David ate, as he fasted and wept before God in his brokenness.

***

Psalm 55:17

"Evening and morning and at noon I will pray, and cry aloud, and He shall hear my voice."

It is as we meditate upon the visual image of David on his knees, weeping before God night and day, that we begin to absorb the true nature of "a broken and contrite heart." We may glean from this passage that David at one stage, or perhaps ongoing for the remainder of his life thereafter, apportioned three segments of time within a given day, to "pray and cry aloud." At best, here in the West, and as we are plagued with the perpetual stress of hyper-activity; we do well to apportion a brief segment in the mornings and evenings to find time to still ourselves with the Lord. David however began his day, realigned his day at midday, and ended his day with praying and crying aloud to God. David's entire day therefore was committed and *sub*mitted to God. It took the riveting and soul-wrenching exposure of his sin to break him of his personal agenda within the context of the average day. It was hereafter that David's days were aligned with overriding focus upon continual dialogue with God.

For many of us, and perhaps most of us; we cannot imagine the liberty of orchestrating our days to evolve around dialogue with God, and to allot three windows in time for doing so. The reality however is that irrespective of the busyness and pressure of our schedules; if we ask Him to reveal such, He will show us just how to sup with Him three times a day, even if but for a few moments. For if He knows when a sparrow falls to the ground (Matthew 10:29), He also knows every facet of the stress, strife and inner turmoil that often plagues our days in the work force. Subsequently, He also knows just when to whisper to us that a divine window in time has been orchestrated, just so that we may momentarily sup with Him, and "cry aloud."

Despite the hideous suffering imposed upon Job, he too was aware that *God* was in turn fully aware of all that plagued Job's mind and emotions from one moment to the next. Job subsequently declared: *"He knows the way I take; when He has tried me, I shall come forth as gold."* God knows the "way we take" in the course of our workweeks; He knows our frailties, our doubts, our stressors, our worries, our fatigue, our frustrations and our points of confusion as they unfold by the hour, and He wishes to be found in every moment, that He may be granted license to order our steps, and to insert peace into our storms. And many of our storms are those of our own making, in and through our failure to perform *teshuvah* ongoing—to turn from the carnal dictates of our flesh from moment to moment, and rather align our thoughts and emotions with His. He has given us the Helper, the Ruach HaKodesh; the Holy Spirit; to help us navigate every moment, of every hour, of every week, of every year, of every decade—for *life*. He offers us a divine romance—and a romance without end.

Chapter Nine

Your Family
שלך המשפחה

Throughout my story, my saga, my journey, I have sought to paint with a broad brushstroke a picture of God's unfathomable mercy and compassion for His children—you included. I have sought to do so largely through affirming His mercy and compassion through both my personal story, and King David's. In so doing I am strongly tempted to alight upon the entirety of the Book of Psalms, perhaps through an exhaustive chapter-by-chapter expositional musing. But to do so would mean a departure from the more pointed purpose in writing this book—that to touch the depths of your heart—from the depths of mine—with the love of God, as you so opt to perform your own measure of *teshuvah* before Him.

As we continue with but a cursory glimpse of David's life, I will touch briefly upon what I believe to be key excerpts of the remainder of the Psalms—excerpts which speak deeply of God's very real availability and nearness to us, and the equally very real potential for our hope, faith, vision and purpose to be completely restored and rekindled looking forward.

In what *should have been* a divine wake-up call for the nation (the U.S.) on the evening of November 6th of 2008; a massive knee-jerk political reaction rather ensued—and it has yet to stop. To this day, as of this writing, more than five years later; millions of Believer's in this country continue to place hope in political parties and corresponding candidates—parties and candidates positioned to offer apparent redemption from the catastrophic excising of the soul of this nation which has continued, fragment-by-fragment, since November 6th of

2008. What saddens me as I consider this, is that the vast majority of the Body of Christ in this nation has failed to see that God's heavy hand of judgment has been released upon this nation in and through, among other things, a veil of deception which has completely enveloped the nation—and which has *in turn* equated to what has occurred not only on the evening of November 6th of 2008, but also on the evening of November 6th of 20<u>12</u>. As such, our collective reaction has been that to look to *secular* means through which to allay our fears—versus that of looking to *God*, and asking Him how it is that we are to respond.

The failure to focus solely upon what *God* is doing, has resulted in a very pointed acceleration of fear and anxiety mounting in the hearts of people throughout the nation. When we then couple mounting fears and anxiety with unresolved and unhealed conditions of the heart, we allow ourselves to be wound tightly, mentally and emotionally, not unlike the very dense rubber-band-ball within the core of golf balls. There is a remedy. In the *macro* context of a proper national response, *teshuvah* is in order—a nation on its knees, beginning first with the *Church*, for *"judgment begins with the house of God"* (1 Peter 4:17). In the *micro* context however, and that in conjunction with our *personal* repentance; let us look briefly at Psalm chapter 55.

David declares in Psalm 55:22, *"Cast your burden on the Lord, and He shall sustain you; He shall never permit the righteous to be moved."* During the previous century millions of psychologists and psychiatrists made subsequent millions of *dollars*, through doing not much more than simply *listening*. As a young psychology major many years ago, a very successful Jungian Therapist mentored me briefly. The sole key for his success (defined in monetary terms *only*) was that of his discipline in refraining from dialogue while listening to his clients. He would place his chin in his hands, nod his head, smile on occasion, and would not flinch when uncomfortable silence would ensue. He knew that more than anything else, his clients simply wanted to be *heard*, and to know that someone was *really* listening. In and through his posture he would force his clients to talk, and keep them talking through systematic smiles and nodding his head—the conveyance of "active listening." He would occasionally interject some secular humanistic psychological mumbo-jumbo while reflecting on a given client's dreams—terribly bypassing the *spiritual* implications of such; and would end his sessions by first ensuring they had arrived at another appointment on the calendar; and secondly, by revisiting the status of a given prescription for anti-depressants and/or sleeping pills. Surly, he authenticated his discipline of offering Jungian Psychology, by elaborating upon his Jungian insights, advice, etc. But his primary offering was that of simply *listening*—even though in his heart he could not have possibly cared less about a given client's life—unless the client happened to be an attractive young *female*. On a redemptive note, I did place a heavy deposit of the reality of Christ in our final conversations as mentor and pupil; the final conversation of which met with a rather violent end through a demonic manifestation on his part.

I believe it important to interject that I believe there is *some* redemptive value to Jung's offerings with respect to the study of type, symbol and metaphor, etc., within dreams. However, if it is not utilized in tandem with the plumb-line of scripture and the filter of authentic spiritual discernment, it can very well lead to *"...vanity of vanities...and striving after the wind...".*

Why would I allude to the example of this therapist? I have done so to underscore the reality that God *Himself* is an "active listener" (far more active than the best-intentioned therapist) and He waits, and waits, and waits for us to come to a place where we want to dialogue with Him, to share all that is on our hearts. We need much more than any available human being who will listen to us passively, thus enabling us to "get a few things off our chest."

We rob ourselves terribly, if we become conditioned to believe that the only way to dialogue with God is that while praying to Him, and worshipping Him, as we understand such in the conventional sense—as important as both of these postures are. For equally so, He is available to us as a *listener*—as one who waits for us to cast our burden upon Him perpetually. What does David mean really, when he declares that *"He shall never permit the righteous to be moved"?* May I offer that what David is referring to, is that of God's promise to never permit us to be moved from our special place of intimacy with Him, His loving embrace, and His ready posture of a Father waiting to listen to us, to take from us all that is weighing heavily upon our hearts and minds. By divine design, external conditions will deeply affect our internal being. But it is not God's design that external conditions eat us alive internally, propelling us to adapt to such by finding less-than-godly outlets and mediums through which to cope.

For most of us, and me included, the turmoil of thoughts and emotions which at times seem to strangle us, often pull us into a figurative cave—a place of hiding from grim realities in our lives. This cave often takes on the form of secret sin as a momentary escape from a harsh reality. David himself, in response to a "harsh reality," found himself retreating into a *literal* cave at one stage in his life, as he fled from King Saul who was bent on destroying him, solely motivated by an insane level of jealousy toward God's favor and anointing upon David's life. From the depths of David's *literal* cave, and when he could have rather opted to medicate himself with much wine, or even have killed himself, he declared, *"I will sing and give praise. Awake, my glory! Awake lute and harp! I will awaken the dawn."*

Consider this picture for a moment: David is on the run from a mad King who wants to kill him; he is sleeping in dirt; he is filthy, and eating whatever wild animals he and his band can capture and kill. His natural response would be that to allow himself to become consumed in depression and hopelessness. And what does he rather do? He commands musical instruments (one of which I believe he could very well have taken with him as he fled—perhaps the ancient equivalent of a "travel-guitar," or harp, in his case) to "awaken!" He also declares that he "will awaken the dawn." David is declaring that he will rise so early in the morning to worship the Lord that he will awaken the dawn even before the dawn *itself* is scheduled to wake up and produce the light to which it is responsible. David had tapped the key to never being "moved" from God's presence—irrespective of the circumstances. David worshipped early in the morning, while it was still dark, a time when most are still deep in their slumber. Consider that God is available, early in the morning; ready and available; and even eager to hear us worship Him in a sleepy stupor, out of key; and even with an alarming case of "bed-hair."

Imagine for a moment, a gentle tug on your arm very early in the morning, while you're sound asleep. You awaken to find a child kneeling next to you with arms outstretched, longing for an embrace. What do you suppose your response to be? Without even thinking about it, and while being overwhelmed with emotion you would embrace them, and say, "I love you." Such is the very same exchange which occurs when we chose to dialogue with God, and to worship Him, when we find ourselves in dark caves. As we lift our arms to Him in worship; when worship defies all that our carnal beings are commanding, He embraces us. As we continue this practice, we find that before long, we're no longer alone in the cave, and at times *removed* from the cave thereafter.

I've personally found that God typically has two primary objects in His intensely personal dealings with us; He is either trying to *remove* something from our hearts which should not be there, or, He is trying to place something *in* our hearts which *should* be there. Sometimes our noncooperation with His agenda lands us in a dark cave. Equally so, sometimes our *full* cooperation entails seasons in the same cave, such as His call to the backside of the desert to die yet further to self. He does not *tempt* us, but He does very often *test* us, as He so did David. The measure to which David continued to humble himself and honor God's servants—even when His servants had temporarily lost their minds; became the commensurate measure to which David would later rule and reign as King. God was clearly forging and honing an area of David's heart which housed the perpetual awareness and acceptance of God's sovereignty—as terrifying as it can be at times. He was also further forging and honing David's resolve to exude a lifestyle of worship—*no matter what.*

David revealed His practice of worshipping God in the early morning throughout the Psalms. In Psalm 59:16 we read, *"...I will sing aloud of your mercy in the morning..."* It continued to matter not the circumstances, for at this stage in David's life he found his sustenance in worshipping God—perpetually. David was posturing what it is that we are soon stepping-into as the Church Universal—the collective Bride of Christ globally. And as we have meditated on such the posture in previous chapters, we continue to meet with this recurring theme. And it is this theme that I will continue to marinate as we look further into several remaining jewels within the treasure chest of David's story.

***

Psalm 68:6(a)

"God sets the solitary in families..."

For those who have entered life as an orphan, whether literally or figuratively, and who have experienced what it means to have no sense of identity with a given family; you know very well this unique brand of pain. Those of you who have then gone on to embrace life in Jesus, have found that He seeks to set you ("the solitary") in a family—a family of like-minded Believers who have one goal—that of loving you, as *He* loves you. Such families are increasingly uncommon at this juncture in Western Church history, but they do exist, and if we will pray for such, He will set us in such a place. Sometimes such the family (congregation) is one that we are being called to birth and lead. I do not doubt many who would read this book will experience a heart-twinge upon reading the previous sentence. If this is you, perhaps you may consider re-reading the previous sentence.

In and through my protracted state of denial as a young Believer, I gave myself over to seasons of delusion—the *fruit* of protracted denial. For in the same way that anger-turned-inward ultimately morphs into depression, so denial, masked long enough, morphs into delusion. In such a state, there are very few who will draw near to us to reach out to us as "family." Very few within our vicinity will muster enough courage to confront delusion in others, as it can get very dirty, and there is simply very little external reward. And we're all looking for external rewards. It is therefore as we choose to deny ourselves, and "go after those staggering to the slaughter," that we are nobly emulating the Father's Heart.

There will be those among the readership of my story, who, not unlike me, have created such a mess relationally at one point in their lives, that wherever they go they simply cannot out-live their failures, for some phantom form of slander has gone before you with every step, and those who newly greet you, in short order flee from you as they learn of your story through other means. I have personally felt such the devastating sting of slander. It can be crippling.

Those of you who have experienced this brand of pain must know that our Adversary capitalizes on such a web of destruction, by seeking to convince us that we will never out-live our past. But you must know dear reader, that as you have fallen at the feet of Jesus, and have confessed your sins to Him, He casts your sin into a sea of forgetfulness. And as you have sought to ask forgiveness of others, and that irrespective of their response, you have done what the Holy Spirit has prodded you to do. If a victim of your wrongdoing chooses to hold you in bondage as the result of unforgiveness toward you, they are in fact holding *themselves* in bondage. You must *choose* freedom, and freedom is in

93

fact, a *choice*.

Irrespective of how alienated you feel as the result of the rubble and refuse you have produced in your wounded state, you must know that as you ask Him, God will place you within a family, a family who will be charged with loving you as you are.

It is difficult for the majority of Believers in the West to comprehend the suffering endured by those who comprise the Underground Church in communist, socialist, and otherwise oppressive nations (the U.S. is soon to follow-suit). *Millions* of very dear and godly Believers have died at the hands of oppressive socialist and communist regimes in recent decades alone. Such persecution and oppression is rapidly escalating presently, and stealthily moving into the West, not unlike a gentle incoming tide steadily lapping at one's bare feet while strolling along the beach. Soon it will not be so gentle.

One such Believer who has suffered severely, is a man who has long served an apostolic role within the underground church in China. This particular brother has suffered forms of torture while in prison which have brought him to within moments of death, on many occasions. As he tells his story, he shares of occasions while imprisoned, when he was within a few seconds of resigning to this life—an act of the will; when the Holy Spirit suddenly flooded his being, and surged him with life. At one point in one of his imprisonments he chose to fast for what has been the longest record that I am aware of, without food and water. In so doing he lost 60% of his body weight, and his ears actually shriveled-up like rotten walnuts due to extreme dehydration. His crime? He was repeatedly arrested for playing a critical leadership role within the underground church at large in China.

During his imprisonment this brother's wife and family nearly starved to death. Local police saw to it that friends and family in the area were prevented from aiding them with food. This saga went on for several years (it is timely to note that oppressive regimes like that in China routinely seek to starve the families of Christian prisoners, by forbidding neighbors and extended family from supporting them). Upon his release, he mourned deeply as he looked into the faces of his wife and children, and saw their pain, their premature aging, their malnourished frames, and their ragged clothes. He could only weep. The price he had paid for his faithful service was beyond what we in the West can fathom. Not long following his release he was asked to speak at a conference in Canada. After making the long journey from Asia to Canada, and only hours after arriving in Canada, he discovered that his booking within the forthcoming conference had been cancelled. When he inquired as to why, he was only told that some very troubling information about him had made its way to the conference organizers, and that he was no longer welcome.

I wept as I read this man's devastating story. He would later learn that a man (but *one* man) had begun sowing slander about this dear brother even before he left Asia bound for Canada. The slanderer told a convincing tale that the brother's story of extreme suffering and imprisonment was fabricated. Our dear Chinese brother would go on to share in his memoir that the pain of the hideous level of slander that had been released against him, was far greater than the pain of his suffering in prison, and the lateral suffering of his family, over many years.

I know dear reader, this form of searing pain, not unlike a glowing-hot poker branding one's skin—the severe toxicity of very carefully calculated slander. It is cancerous, and grows and grows, often never stopping. My name has been assaulted beyond measure in this regard. As I share this, I know that there are those who will read my story, and who will identify with this crippling assault. For these; perhaps you have felt you would never again be accepted and loved within a family of Believers, because of the sweltering trail of pain as the result of the assignation of your character. If this is you, know that as you ask Him, God will place you in a family who will embrace you irrespective of your sordid trail. His

95

mercies are new every morning, and it is up to us to arise early enough in the morning to fetch them, not unlike fetching freshly laid eggs from the hen house.

Chapter Ten

A Day in His Courts
שלו המשפט בבתי יום

As I look back upon my 33-year experience with
Western Christianity, I find myself poised to pen a series
of books which speak to the "800-pound gorilla" in the
sanctuary—the gorilla that most people artfully and
sheepishly tip-toe around as they make their way to the
same seat they've *always* sat in, in public meetings. The
gorilla to which I allude is named *Spiritual Narcissism*—
the obsessive focus upon one's *self*. We have bred such,
here in the West. In and through such breeding we have
created tens of millions of Believers who have wallowed in
self-pity for much of their adult lives, "recovering" from
one wound or another—as a lifestyle representative of a
growing church subculture. We have in turn created
thousands of Recovery Programs, designed to help people
"recover." Most of these recovery programs initially begin
to serve fruitful ends. However, very often and very
quickly many participants succumb to defining
themselves *by* their recovery program; this is where we
can cross a thin-red-line, as we transition from pure
heart-motivation, to utter self-absorption.

Having observed the fruits of such programs over
33 years, as well has having participated in a great many
myself, and leading many, I have first observed that many
who have written books and programs around such have
gone on to become quite successful (monetarily)—using
mega-churches and associated media streams as their
primary marketing venues. I have secondly observed that
with rare exception, most Believers that I know who have
been involved in recovery programs for most of their
Christian lives have managed to artfully avoid and mask a

core issue—that of *un-forgiveness*; which, over a lifetime morphs into bitterness, and becomes a deeply embedded bitter-root; following which corresponding health issues of every sort manifest, both psychological and emotional. To compound matters, one can easily become self-deluded over time into believing that the wound of but *one person* is responsible for all that does not line-up in one's life. I believe this widespread tragedy to be rooted in one very simple mistake—that of taking our eyes off the *Cross of Jesus*, and the *Blood* of Jesus. Therefore, wherever we meet with a venue or congregation which taboos mention of "the Cross" and "the Blood," we will in turn meet with a large number of people in deep bondage, for it is the very *Cross* and the *Blood* that have the power to free us from the deepest traumas to the soul—and the subsequent bondage such trauma can create (I strongly encourage the reader to re-read this sentence).

Please understand, dear reader, that I fully acknowledge the merits and benefits of recovery programs and corresponding groups similar. The benefits of immediate fellowship (i.e., fellowship within the context of a given meeting), is chief among these merits. Fellowship, or group interaction, fosters ministry to one another and serves fruitful ends; most especially that of the act of praying for one another. But please understand that equally, the typical dynamics within recovery groups also foster the coddling of our personal demons—namely the demons of un-forgiveness, self-pity and narcissism. Very often such programs, groups and corresponding meetings equate to one colorfully protracted pity-party, wherein we not only convince all in attendance that the perpetrator of our personal wounds is a monster; we also further convince *ourselves* of the same, yet further cementing our hardened heart, and our deeply-seated resolve to "milk" the trauma for all its worth—all the while secretly retaining a heart-posture of un-forgiveness deep within— artfully masked with false-humility and hyper-spirituality.

David declared in Psalm 71:6, *"By You I have been upheld from birth; You are He Who took me out of my mother's womb..."* This one verse speaks deeply to me personally, as I survived an assault upon my life which occurred while I was yet in my mother's womb. In fact therefore, it was God *"...Who took me out of my mother's womb."* I am inclined to believe that King David could have very well experienced a demonic assault upon his life while still in the womb. We are not told in definitive terms. We can assume however that David realized without God's deliverance from evil David would have never met the light of day. Satan is not omnipotent, however I'm fully convinced that his original divine attributes, though wholly perverted upon his fall, include that of the ability to see prophetically to a degree; to see with linear perspective what is unfolding within a given genealogical story; and to subsequently seek to thwart God's purposes therein, to include assaults upon those still in the womb—as well as those freshly without the womb.

Having survived the initial assault upon *my* life, I thereafter began to wrestle with the greatest "personal demon" I've encountered in my lifetime—*rejection.* Having since ministered to thousands of Believers who have wrestled with the same for much of their adult lives, I've come to conclude that there is but *one* "recovery program" that works. The program in question is this: *intimacy with God.* As we press-in to further know Him with each day, we come to know that He will not reject us as we draw near to Him with a heart of contrition. As we do so, He *affirms* us. And each time He affirms us, He further burns-away that beast of rejection. Until we learn to press-in to know Him intimately, daily, we will fall prey to seeking to fill our personal affirmation-void (spawned by rejection) with other mediums, which are expressed in a variety of ways, all of which are destructive to our souls.

We often harbor strongholds of deeply-seated anger and bitterness rooted in a deep rejection-wound. We seek to fill this wound, and associated void, with affirmation from others. We also seek affirmation of our perceived "personal right" and "entitlement" to harbor anger, resentment, and hurt. We can do a fine job of convincing others—and ourselves—that this is a noble undertaking—

a life pursuit; but we fool ourselves as we do so.

As expressed moments ago; though many of the primary tenets of a myriad of recovery programs and systems in the West have merit, and that chiefly the benefit of the potential for facilitating authentic fellowship, which I whole-heartedly endorse; the primary tenets are most often jeopardized by a fog of spiritual narcissism—and the quest to prove to the world about us that it is our "personal right" to be angry, resentful, depressed, bitter; and to remain a victim; to be *known* as a victim—to find our identity as a victim—to cultivate a perpetual pity-party—and to feed the monster—the demon—which convinces us that we are justified in thereafter slandering and maligning those who've wounded us—not only keeping *them* in bondage, but keeping *ourselves* in bondage as the result.

Psalm 71:20 declares: *"You, Who have shown me great and severe troubles, shall revive me again, and bring me up again from the depths of the earth."* God shows us "great and severe troubles" by merely *allowing* great and severe troubles to come our way. Many of our severe troubles are demonic, and God often allows demonic forces to run their course in our lives as the result of generational sins and iniquities sown before us. He equally allows such to run their course in our lives as the result of our *personal* sins and iniquities. Irrespective, as we continue to press-in to know Him in and through daily intimacy, it is *He* Who will also *"bring* [you] *up again from the depths of the earth"* – *not* a recovery program. There is simply no substitute for daily intimacy with the Lord.

There are those who will no doubt take offense to my less-than-glorious expose' of recovery programs, systems and networks. Before allowing such an offense to further grow roots however, please allow me to share a grossly overlooked segment of history with you—a segment of history which powerfully underscores my point—and a segment of history which may enable you to see things a bit differently.

For nearly 60 years, there was believed to have been an estimated 6 million Jews murdered during the

Nazi Holocaust, as well as an untold number of "Jewish-Sympathizers" (i.e., non-Jews who happened to have harbored the rare combination of love and courage). In recent years, the larger death toll, which includes those non-Jews who aided fleeing Jews, and who perished in death camps, is said to be more like *25 million.* The more famous death camps, such as those depicted in the more renowned dramas in theaters over the past few decades, have been determined to represent but a small fraction of the actual number of death camps. For the Jews and Jewish-Sympathizers who survived the Nazi death camps, it was rare that any of them would find a surviving family member thereafter. Consider therefore, the mental and emotional state of a Jewish survivor of Nazi death camp, who then discovers that their entire family has been murdered. Bear in mind that as they have exited virtual hell on earth, and are psychologically and emotionally numbed beyond words as the result, they are met with the reality that they are the only surviving family member. Even worse, many of them would discover that their entire villages had been completely wiped off the map—and with no known survivors. To *further* compound their trauma, they are whisked to various "Displaced Person's Camps" (wherein each survivor was thereafter dubbed a "DP") by the United Nations Relief and Rehabilitation Administration (later replaced by the International Refugee Organization). The camps were organized throughout Europe, and the "DP's" often pined-away for extended periods while the authorities rubbed their chins and scratched their heads, wondering what to do with them. Many of them were fortunate to have been placed in homes abroad, yet many would also remain in the camps for more than a year, without family, no income, and no foreseeable future. For these, their only hope and dream (often deeply instilled in them by their parents beforehand) would be that to return to Zion—to Israel—their ancestral home, and to find a resting place therein.

In time, many would then find the means to leave the camps and make their way to Israel on ships, living in squalid conditions in the lower decks while in route. Following several years of collective suffering and hardship, and after setting out for Israel with nothing more than a bundle on their backs; many of these would meet with the *unthinkable*—that of being turned away from the Israeli shore. Many ships were turned-back by British military, and forced to return to Europe, with thousands of heart-broken Jews aboard. The British military had mandated a limit upon those permitted ashore to obtain citizenship in the Promised Land. Many of these who then survived yet *another* harrowing trip back to Europe while continuing to live in squalid conditions aboard the ships, would then ultimately make their way back to Israel on yet *another* ship. Those who then ultimately made it to Israeli soil, and just when some semblance of new life began to materialize before them, not long thereafter met with a violent assault comprised of every Arab state surrounding the tiny state, and not unlike a pack of rabid wolves, pouncing upon Israel in an attempt to destroy the nation as it was then *pronounced* a nation. Therefore, even before these desperate holocaust survivors had the chance to begin a new life, a rifle was thrown in their hands and they found themselves once again *fighting for their lives.*

I ask you, dear reader; *when* did these holocaust survivors have the luxury of attending a Recovery Group? *When* did they have the luxury of staging a pity-party, and groveling in their wounds and obsessing over their tormentors? Those who then survived the *next* war, the War of 1948, only had but *one* option—that of *beginning a new life.* Most went on to find mates and create new families in short order. They avenged their tormenters by *living*—and by starting new lives, by creating new life. Upon Israel's impossible victory in 1948, most of these survivors could be seen dancing in the streets in circles, performing the "Horah," while singing "Hava Nagila" as they celebrated the defeat of the neighboring Arab states. The same people who had survived hell on earth in death camps, and later in the form of squalid conditions on ships; fought in vicious gorilla-like combat from street-to-street in Jerusalem, often with no training beforehand; then found themselves dancing in the streets as Israel is liberated.

As a student of holocaust literature for a number of years now, I am tempted to share at length the stories of many holocaust survivors; for many excerpts of books and articles, accounts and memoirs will never leave me. For the moment I will share but one brief excerpt of a story which took place at Auschwitz, one of three of the most notorious death camps. As I do so, understand that I am not simply offering the reader an interesting glimpse of history, but much more so seeking to underscore a substantial point that I hope will never leave you.

A train arrives at Auschwitz, loaded with thousands of terrified Jews who have been crammed into box cars like cattle. For days they lived in such conditions, and with no food, water or toiletries; forced to relieve themselves in a corner with a bucket, in full view of hundreds of others. With no food, water, nor sleep, many of the elderly, sick, and babies, died en route. As the train arrived at Auschwitz, families were torn from one another. In the ensuing chaos a young teenage girl who would go on to survive the camp and tell of her experience, recalls stumbling about, mentally numbed, as families are crying and screaming as they are separated by Nazi guards. In shock, she has lost her equilibrium and finds herself walking alone, perhaps 25 yards or more from the ensuing malaise. She is unnoticed for the moment, by the guards who have their hands full. She looks upward at smoke stacks billowing a kind of smoke she has never seen before. She then looks downward and sees subsurface concrete ramps loaded with people who are being prodded into the lower level of the building. Immediately she intuits that these people were being gassed and incinerated; she had heard the stories, and was now seeing the reality unfold before her eyes. As she stares at the people stumbling into the building, she sees the shock, terror and resignation in their faces. In her traumatic stupor, and as she blankly stares at the people slowly walking toward their deaths, a woman older than she, from within the crowd marching into the building, turns her face toward the young onlooker, and shouts: *"Avenge us!"*

The young teen would never forget this moment as long as she lived. She would go on to "avenge" the death of millions—by *living*. She would also go on to avenge the death of the woman who charged her with such, by leading countless people to the study of Torah, and by keeping the flame of Judaism alive. Lastly, she would avenge the death of millions by speaking truth, and refusing to ignore oppression—wherever it surfaced.

I've shared this brief account of Auschwitz, dear reader, to in turn share that we avenge our tormentors by *living*, by speaking *truth*—especially about *ourselves*; by sharing with others our known path to God, and by being a bearer of light in the midst of oppressive darkness. We do not avenge our tormentors by obsessing over our wounds. We in the West however have made such the full-time obsession; we have created an entire *industry* of it. I have been personally guilty of such the obsession. I have subsequently sought to walk in *teshuvah*—repentance.

***

Psalm 84:10

"For a day in Your courts is better than a thousand outside. I would rather stand at the threshold of the house of my God, than dwell in the tents of wickedness."

What do we suppose this "court" to be, that David alludes to? I suggest that it is simply that of God's unmistakable presence—the place where He *dwells*. This could be within the walls of a given sanctuary or synagogue, or it could be any kind of informal meeting place where saints gather to worship. I tend to believe the court's to which David alludes, are the *courts of praise*—wherever praise happens to occur. As God inhabits the praises of His people; we find that He dwells wherever we so choose to praise Him—in spirit and in truth.

Throughout the beautiful tapestry of worship woven into the fabric of the Book of Psalms, we are often met with images of David dancing in his palace, worshiping God, wholly oblivious to onlookers stationed in the palace, or beyond. I do not doubt that he was deemed a madman on many occasions, perhaps for appearing to dance with an imaginary figure. When God's presence becomes more tangible to us than the physical objects around us however, the figure with whom we are dancing is no longer imaginary.

I recall many years ago observing a man who would worship God during public worship services in such a way that it appeared he was dancing ballroom style, with an imaginary figure. My worship posture was a bit more reserved at the time, but no less intimate. The worship services in this venue, at the time, hosted 1,000 people or more, and worship would sometimes go on for over an hour, maybe more. God's presence would so fill the venue that people would freely express their worship without inhibition. Many personalities stood-out however, some of whom were subject to subtle ridicule, albeit humorous and seemingly harmless jesting. Truly, we need to learn to laugh at ourselves often, and to also have thin-skin as others laugh at us as well, but in this instance the ballroom-style worship flowing through this man was a holy affair. It reflected his complete abandonment to Jesus, and to worshipping Him with his whole being, irrespective of who was watching and what they were thinking and saying. And it is this measure of abandonment to Jesus, and intimacy with Him, that we will be granted precious privilege to become increasingly familiar *with*, as we learn to daily dwell in His "courts."

As we worship, and as we look skyward during worship, we completely lose sight of our "issues." We completely lose sight of our guilt, condemnation, remorse; our depression, our loneliness, our confusion and our pain. And as the Lord responds to our worship He often blankets us in such a way with His Holy Spirit that a trigger of godly sorrow begins to well-up as the result of unresolved sin. As our tears begin to subsequently flow, we are washed in a river of His cleansing—the River of Life. We are also washed of the strongholds of scars associated with personal traumas. It is in this place, His "courts," that the sting of our circumstances, hideous as they may be, will pale in contrast to the glimpse of glory we glean while yielding the fullness of our beings to Him, in worship.

Throughout thousands of public meetings I have attended over a 33-year period; many in which I was honored to have been asked to speak; I can recall like it was yesterday, the unique and powerful expression of the Holy Spirit's presence. In one such meeting my wife and I were graced to experience the personal testimony and heart-riveting story of an apostolic figure who suffered terribly for his ministry in Vietnam and Cambodia decades ago. Subjected to unspeakable suffering, he was once imprisoned in a muddy hole in the ground which was covered by a woven bamboo hatch. In this muddy pit, he had no toiletries. He had to relieve himself in his squalor. He had no outlet in which to bathe. He nearly starved to death, while being fed rancid water and rotten bread. His muddy pit was like an oven during the day, contrasted by cold rains which would pelt him at night and create of puddle of mud and squalor reaching close to his knees. He would shiver throughout the night uncontrollably. On one such evening, cold, shivering, soaked, and starving; and feeling the agonizing gnawing in his heart over not knowing the whereabouts of his wife and children; he decided to begin worshipping. He began singing, *"I've got a river of life flowing out of me; makes the lame to walk and the blind to see; opens prison doors, sets the captives free, I've got a river of life flowing out of me."* Within moments, the entirety of his being was numbed to his suffering as he sang. He then felt his muddy pit become flooded with God's presence, and he was granted an open-vision of angels singing along with him. To test what he was seeing and hearing, he stopped singing for a moment—long enough to hear the angels singing without him. Not long thereafter he was freed, and was subsequently re-united with his wife and children. Never forget this truth, dear reader: it was his decision to worship God in the worst conceivable circumstances, that so *moved* the heart of God that He would miraculously set the man free. This brother had discovered that worship *is our warfare*—the most potent weapon at our disposal.

There are those who taboo the personal experience of open-visions, heavenly visitations, and unusual encounters with God; encounters that are outside of *their* personal experience. For these, most have been prevented from experiencing such through the sting of sterile theology—theology that purports the cessation of such experiences with the divine. Theology and Doctrine in my lifetime have done more to *suppress* intimacy with God, than they have to present the initial reality of God to the lost soul. For once a lost soul has managed to survive the maze of Western theology and doctrine, they are very fortunate if they manage to encounter the likes of Jesus along the way. Please understand that I've "done my time" in the theology and doctrine department, as a post-graduate student of the same. I've earned a few letters behind my name in so doing, but such "formal" study has done nothing to draw me closer to Jesus. I earned the letters to simply satisfy my critics. *Meditating* upon scripture, versus *studying* scripture, enables us to be transformed as we read. Otherwise we simply fill our heads with theological trivia laced with handsome religious platitudes.

Though we welcome confusion and even delusion when we make it our sole focus to have unusual encounters with the Lord; we equally welcome confusion and delusion if we *deny* that they can occur. God is the God of creativity, and He creatively meets with each of us in ways unique to anyone else. As He meets with us, and as He draws near when we completely abandon ourselves to His ways and means—to the symphony of the mysterious ebb and flow of the Holy Spirit, we can be removed from the rubble and squalor of the worst places of suffering, and thereafter be placed in His "courts"; in His presence; where we are further transformed to the likeness of Jesus. It is also in this place that in and through our heart-posture of contrition, humility and brokenness, our steps can be divinely guided in such a way that we find the grace to fully welcome His divine restoration of our lives, no matter how messy they have become. Equally, our steps are subsequently guided in speaking His restoration into the lives of *others*.

Our souls are watered when we water the souls of others. King Solomon said accordingly, *"He who waters will himself be watered"* (Proverbs 11:25). It is as we repent, as we embrace *teshuvah* for our vain focus upon ourselves, and rather focus upon others, that we very often meet with a mysterious brand of healing.

Chapter Eleven

I Called Upon Him
לעליו התקשרתי

It was roughly eight years ago that I penned an
article which spoke to a very subtle and subsequently
very effectively *deceptive* strategy to rob human beings of
the ability to still themselves in a quiet place long enough
to discern the presence of God—and the *voice* of God. As
I penned such, I spoke to the average time within the
context of a given day, that the average American spends
absorbed *in and by* some audio-visual device, be it a
laptop, desktop PC, Smartphone, big-screen TV, car
radio, home radio, iPod, MP3-player, etc. Some eight
years later, it is truly staggering to ponder the audio-
visual-system-overload that consumes both the minds
and emotions of the average American. Such the plague
has equated to, among other things, pronounced
superficiality and confusion within all ranks of Western
society—to include the *pulpit*. The reality is that it is
simply impossible to allow such daily saturation of our
minds, without also in turn incurring the *reshaping* of our
minds. One very pronounced side effect of such the
dynamic for example, is the frequency with which I hear
most Americans interpreting national political issues
through grossly distorted lenses which have been molded
by gravely deceptive mass-media. For at this state in
Western history, there are an extreme few media
companies who are dedicated to fostering truth. These few
are presently under federal scrutiny, and will, in due
season, be forced to muffle their microphones.

I for one am wired for extreme sensitivity, in every
regard, be it sensitivity to foods, various fabrics, noise
levels, imagery, etc. I must for example wear 100% cotton

or wool, otherwise my skin breaks-out in rashes when I
wear synthetically mixed fabrics. In similar fashion, as I
view movies, videos, theater, etc., I must be very cautious.
The same is true of the music I listen to. As a musician
this one is a particular challenge. In my selectivity I seek
to discern the *spirit* behind a given movie for example. In
the past few decades I've fared well in sniffing-out jewels
among movies; most of them dramas. Though few and far
between, each one has left a lasting impact upon me. One
such movie is that entitled *Sense and Sensibility,* a movie
depicting late eighteenth century high-society England,
and chronicling the triumphs and heartaches within the
saga of the Dashwood family, who go from riches, to near-
rags, and back to riches again through many heart-
wrenching episodes. The story follows the Dashwood
daughters, and their quest for true love. Emerging from
the story are three men who pursue the two oldest
daughters, Elinor and Marianne.

Two of the three men who emerge, embody all that
is noble. The third of the three is a handsome, dashing
and yet highly divisive man (John Willoughby).
Willoughby is divisive in that he never comes to terms
with his past, and paints a very convincing social charade
that fools most, but leaves some a little uneasy, as they
intuit something which is "not quite right" about him. The
two *true* noblemen are represented in Colonel Brandon
and Edward Ferrars. Ultimately, Colonel Brandon marries
Marianne Dashwood and Mr. Edward Farrars marries
Elenor Dashwood, but not without a great deal of
heartache in between; inclusive of the heartache spawned
by one John Willoughby, who manages to remain just
ahead of his sordid past throughout the story, until the
very end; and who ultimately forsakes his love for
Marianne to preserve a fortune represented in another
woman—a woman he doesn't love.

My brief narrative of *Sense and Sensibility* does the
movie little justice. My aim in alluding to the film is that
of meditating upon the paradox represented in Edward
Ferrars and John Willoughby. An element of this very
paradox is also mirrored in Herman Hesse's novel,

Narcissus and Goldman, wherein we observe the life of a young seminary student who withdraws from an intensive study of theology, to engage many years of wanderlust and illicit relationships, only to wind up back in the presence of his befriended seminary professor, Narcissus; when they then discuss at length Goldman's journey.

It is Goldman's journey that so uncannily underscores the reality of the perpetual war between our carnal nature and our spirits. The Apostle Paul underscores this war in Romans 7:23-24: *"...I see a different law in the members of my body, waging war against the law of my mind and making me a prisoner of the law of sin which is in my members. Wretched man that I am! Who will set me free from the body of this death?"*

Though I am tempted to expand further upon the merits of Hesse's work herein, I will briefly return to the purpose of my allusion to the *Sense and Sensibility* story.

Edward Ferrars' character is one of timidity, introversion, quietness and gentleness. His character represents the essence of what God has sought to fashion in *me* since childhood—since before I was born. As the result of violence and fear consuming my life early on however, I was propelled to mask who God has created me to be, through an exterior or toughness. I had also managed to artfully mask my deepest wounds through the manufacturing of charisma and the ability to convince people into believing that I was "together," when I was nothing more than fragments—being held together by just a few threads. Throughout my lifetime, when I have met with venues graced with God's peace, I've taken liberty to exhale, to let my guard down, and to be who I have been created to be. And when I do, I very much find myself mirroring the character of Edward Ferrars. As I saw *Sense and Sensibility* for the first time, I wept, as I saw in Edward some semblance of who I am beneath a thick protective and defense layer. To the cold contrary, I also saw in the character of John Willoughby what I had allowed myself to *become* during many seasons in my life, to stay above being found out, by masking my deepest wounds and the trail of tears they had created in the lives of others.

One of the overriding forces that kept me in the throes of bondage to my past, is that of the Religious Spirit lacing much of mainstream Christianity in this nation presently. This to say, that it is very rare that I've had the liberty to be completely transparent about my past in the presence of others, without also incurring immediate judgment and condemnation. This reality is a telling commentary on where the Church in the West is, presently. This dynamic keeps Believers in bondage—one of the more effective strategies of the many tentacles that comprise the monster represented in the Religious Spirit.

As a former and formal student of psychology, and subsequent formal and *informal* student of human behavior in general ongoing for many years, I have long marveled at the much-heralded academic contributions of many notable psychiatrists and psychologists. At best, and for the most part, their collective scientific and academic findings are a feeble attempt at defining and understanding the evil inherent in human beings. Evil, as in *demons*. And until the Blood of Jesus is applied to our evil, we will continue to wear masks of many flavors— flavors which will continue to baffle the "experts." One such "mask" as coined in the psychiatric community, is that defined in general within the field of Psychopathology. A chief contributor to this field in the past century is the late Dr. Hervey Cleckley, who penned among other works, a book entitled *The Mask of Sanity*, which represents an in-depth study of those exuding sociopathic behavior, among related diagnoses. As convincing as the book is academically, it yet completely misses the epicenter of the condition and subsequent remedy—the condition being that of *demonized*—the only remedy being the *Blood of Jesus*. Secular-humanistic "therapy" combined with psychotropic mediation does nothing to dislodge demons. In fact, it *feeds* them, much like handing a full bag of Oreo cookies to an obese ten year old.

Whenever I see a post-middle-aged man with silver hair and a pot-belly, putting down the road in a '50's or

'60's era muscle car that has exacted perhaps a decade or more of time away from his wife to build the car, as well as a significant chunk of what should have been placed in savings; I often quip to anyone who happens to be with me at the time: *"Low self-esteem manifests itself in very colorful ways, does it not?"* Most who drive such vehicles in post-middle-age often suffer from an ongoing case of mild whiplash—as their heads perpetually dart about while driving these vehicles—seeking to make eye contact with as many people possible, to absorb fleeting "hits" of affirmation from those who envy and lust after the vehicle. This practice is not unlike a junkie snaking about in a party, seeking to snort, swallow or shoot-up any and every available high throughout the life of the party. Men are starved for affirmation when their inner lives are in turmoil, and will stoop to laughable means to have their ego's stroked—means about as dignified as the posture of cowboys who lick the bellies of poisonous toads to gain a temporary high from their venom.

The older I get, and perhaps more pointedly, the older I get in the *Lord,* the more grace I feel to simply be myself, and to discard the outer trappings of a phantom exterior. The more I settle into my natural weakness, the more I observe the Holy Spirit moving on my behalf, making me strong in the spiritual where I am weak in the natural. It has taken me nearly a lifetime to discover that when we are weak, we are actually *strong*—a truth spoken by Jesus Himself, and cited by Apostle Paul in 2 Corinthians 12:9: *"...My power is made perfect in weakness."* As we therefore discard the trappings and confines of who we're expected to be socially, and who we've been subsequently led to believe we *should be* socially; and we cease to project something that we are not, thus settling-into who we were uniquely created to be, the Holy Spirit is then released to move freely about our being and further mold us into a unique agent of His glory.

Am I suggesting that the Holy Spirit is *bound* to some degree? I am indeed ("Heresy!" — you retort, but read on...). As long we continue to carryon a convincing charade, and more pointedly a *religious* charade, His hands are tied with respect to His liberty to continue to mold us into the being we were uniquely created to be. You'll get extra credit in heaven if you re-read that sentence.

David Yonggi Cho, senior leader of the largest congregation in the world, a congregation of some 850,000-plus members at this stage, in Seoul South Korea; once stated while speaking at a leadership conference: *"Jesus is bound by our lips."* Cho was immediately lambasted and charged with heresy by multitudes who were *themselves* bound by theology (Apologetics, to be more specific). What Cho was getting at however, is that our words can evoke and further facilitate the Holy Spirit's presence about us, or they can push Him away, leaving the atmosphere sterile and lifeless. The Holy Spirit, Who has often and aptly been referred to as "a Gentleman," will not force Himself upon us nor barge into our circumstances—unless we *invite* Him—and unless we throw-down our guard and remain real and vulnerable with Him. Yonggi Cho, therefore, was truly *onto* something as he stirred-up a religious hornet's nest in his midst.

I have visited and spoken/ministered in many congregations around the country, over many years. On many occasions I've met with such lifeless and sterile atmospheres (the unmistakable trademarks of the dragon named the Religious Spirit) that I found myself struggling to breathe within my first few minutes of speaking—as if the religious spirit was choking me around the neck (actual *physical* feelings of being choked). In such circumstances I've learned that this "dragon" releases his grip and tucks his tail and vacates when I simply begin to tell a story about my frailties, my failures, my struggles with various sins, and how the Lord has subsequently delivered and healed me. It is truly amazing, the immediate change in the spiritual atmosphere when those behind the pulpit or speaking/ministering to a congregation otherwise, are vulnerable and transparent, opening their hearts to all present; hiding nothing. This is a struggle for many onlookers, as the same have been programmed to expect super-human beings and rock stars behind pulpits—those who make a living by positioning and posturing themselves as hyper-spiritual beings, waxing eloquent theologically and *"...taking their stand upon dreams and visions* [often fabricated] *they've had..."* (Col. 2:18), only to conclude such by rendering a candy-coated "word of prophecy" to the senior pastoral team, that the "love offering" tallied moments thereafter might be met with an otherwise unexpected boost.

Say, I haven't forgotten you "muscle car" enthusiasts; I know you're still steaming at me. Lest you seek my address to burn my house down; allow me to render a disclaimer by iterating that I fully realize there are those who enjoy the hobby, and who exemplify the hobby in the spirit of pure fun and appreciation of the magnificent machines they are. But for every *one* of these, there are *nine* others who are desperately in need of personal affirmation, and seek such through public attention—by flaunting their toys. The reader: *"Ah, but David, you've only divulged to us that you have long repressed a secret desire to have a 'muscle car' of your own!"* Actually, I'd rather opt to add another American-made *Fender Stratocaster* to my guitar collection, perhaps an "AVRI '62" in "Tobacco Sunburst" (American Vintage Re-Issue). I think we can safely call it "even" at this stage.

As we succumb to the lures of our flesh, and allow ourselves to be coaxed out from under God's grace, we delay His magnificent plan for our lives and we war against the divine metamorphosis affected within our interior that began when we asked Jesus to make our hearts His home. It is very often that as we wantonly strut headlong into our personal vices of choice, God very often allows goads (figurative stones) to appear within our paths, wherein we perpetually stub our toes until we've had quite enough. He has allowed many goads to be strewn about *my* path over many years, as I have allowed rejection and subsequent anger and the wounds that have propelled them, to dictate my life. As I have done so, I have with ignorance stepped out from under the protective shadow of God's wings, which are so beautifully described in Psalm 91. Verse 1 reads: *"He who dwells in the shelter* [also rendered "secret place"] *of the Most High shall abide under the shadow of the Almighty."*

What is this "shelter" or "hiding place," that we can actually choose to dwell therein? The Hebrew word for "shelter" rendered in this verse, reads "cether" (סֵתֶר), and means literally, *"a secret hiding place."* And it is the secret hiding place that we can run to each time we sup with the Lord, as we discipline ourselves to carve-out time with Him, daily; time *alone* with Him; time spent talking to Him, and listening to Him, in a heart-posture of brutal honesty with ourselves, and with Him. It is herein, in this precious exchange, that we are freed from the trappings of our alter egos, and the facades that we hide behind— the facades which have served us well as seeming survival tools for much of our lives. But have we really survived, without intimacy with Him? If all that we have become is that which correlates with the long-standing effectiveness of our masks, we have anything *but* survived; we have much rather welcomed and effected the suppression of who we've been created to *be*. What can be a greater privilege than that to abide under the shadow of the Almighty?

As I look back upon the many years that I have squandered, often while enmeshed in an admixture of deep anger, rejection, guilt and confusion, I can easily become crippled with grief. Very often the tendency to dwell in the past is that of the prodding of the Evil One, to keep us so fixed upon our rearview mirrors that we cannot effectively drive the vehicles of our lives in a forward motion. We can discipline ourselves against this tendency, by daily absorbing a glimpse of what lay *ahead* of us. And we cannot gain this glimpse without precious time with the One who has written the very script.

As I look about me, in my proximity here in the West, I witness the likeness of a very subtle incoming tide of fear, anxiety and hopelessness, lapping at our feet as we stand barefooted in the sand looking out upon a horizon of apparent doom. The reality is that our nation (the U.S.) is under severe judgment at present—a form of judgment which has allowed wanton evil to run its course in the White House like never before in my lifetime, destroying the very fabric of our national foundation. In very simple terms, what God is allowing to happen to our nation, is that designed to bring us to our knees in humble repentance and contrition. And until the Bride of Christ in this nation repents in concert, the judgment will continue to intensify. As we, as Believers, repent therefore individually, and in growing numbers, we more so begin to represent the *collective* Bride of Christ in a posture of repentance—*teshuvah*. And it is *teshuvah* that we are called-to in this hour, far above all else.

It was thirteen years ago, as of this writing, that through a violent chain of events I began to experience a neurological condition known as *Tinnitus*, a condition which typically entails the torment of ringing, screeching, buzzing or whooshing sounds perpetually in one's head. In my case, I sustained five neck injuries within an 18-month period, which spawned the brand of tinnitus that I suffer (a piercing screech, and which is categorized as "catastrophic tinnitus"—the worst stage). It was during this period that my wife and I were leading a new congregation on an actual island, on the eastern seaboard. Witchcraft, voodoo and freemasonry had consumed the island—all of which made themselves very present in opposition to us—in ways which would raise the hair on the heads of most—leaving them looking not unlike a troll doll, were they to understand the true nature of what we faced in the spirit-realm.

Not long into our new "church-plant" we discovered within the duplex rental in which we lived at the time, that we were sharing one whole wall with a very high-level witch. As she discovered that we were leading a Christian congregation, she began casting spells, hexes and vexes over our duplex, and over our lives. We were in effect blind-sided by her antics, and it was shortly after she began her antics that I experienced the succession of five neck injuries, which ultimately spawned the most severe level of tinnitus possible.

"But David, (you may query)*; does not Luke 10:19, among many other excerpts of scripture, reveal to us that we walk in great authority over such forces?"* Indeed, we *do* walk in such authority. That is, when we are in daily alignment with the ebb-n-flow of the Holy Spirit's gentle prodding, as well as "*dying* daily," as so demonstrated by the early disciples, and the millions of martyrs that have since followed their footsteps. For you see dear reader, I rather choose a return to *dis*obedience during the height of the aforementioned spiritual warfare over my wife and me. God subsequently nudged us out from under the shadow of His wings, and allowed me to once again feel the full brunt of the forces levied against me.

It was during our church-plant hiatus that the psychological and emotional strain wrought of extreme levels of *authentic* spiritual warfare, nudged me into such a haggard state that I dropped my spiritual guard, and allowed the former heart-wounds to surface, and to govern me in such a way that I fell prey to their dictates in the form of anger, bitterness, confusion, emotional turmoil, and compromise.

For those of you who have been in public meetings with microphones present; you may recall your occasional experience with the *piercing* screech of microphone feedback. It is difficult to forget the nature of such hideous noise, as most immediately place their hands over their ears and cringe. It is this very sound that I have lived with, 24 hours a day, for13 years at this stage. It is difficult to describe the mental and emotional battle I face around the clock as the result. I have for 13 years equally refrained from succumbing to the many anti-depressant and sleep medications that my doctors have repeatedly suggested I take, in their concern for my mental health in the wake of such suffering, for most who suffer at my level struggle with very real temptations to commit suicide. I have to date chosen to decline medication, as I have found, through very brief experimentation, that all forms of medication, especially those psychotropic in nature, dull my spiritual sensitivities—preventing me from clearly hearing the still, small voice of the Holy

Spirit. It is God's daily grace in my life that has afforded me the steady stream of peace that sustains me, and which fuels my faith to believe that I will one day meet with a healing balm. His grace also grants me a measure of spiritual equilibrium that prevents me from fully yielding to the hideous mental onslaught associated with catastrophic tinnitus.

The Lord dealt very sternly with me during the tail end of that church plant, speaking to me in no uncertain terms about the dangers of compromise as a Christian leader. It is my firm conviction at this stage, that my refusal to heed the Lord's repeated warnings during this period in turn prompted Him to lift His hand of grace over my life, which allowed the demonic incantations of my neighboring witch to run their full course, the fruits of which have equated to unspeakable suffering as the result of the severe tinnitus condition which has plagued me for so long.

It has taken me many years, and my submitting to multiple deliverance ministry teams yet *again* in my quest for healing, to realize that the tinnitus will leave me only when God Himself has been swayed to heal me. I have had *thousands* of prayers prayed over me, and have endured hundreds of disturbing conclusions made about my condition—construed by neo-Pentecostal theologians—not just "rubbing salt in the wound," but going one step further—by rubbing *battery acid* in the wound.

Many will find fault with the theological self-analysis of my affliction. For these, I offer a little theology in *exchange*, by alluding to a very sobering excerpt of scripture from the "back of the book," in the form of a terrifying warning to the Church in Thyatira; which happens to contain a direct prophetic application to the current Church in the West. And as you read the following excerpt, I challenge you to prayerfully meditate on such if you presently find yourself ensnared by the trappings of pornography, lust, or adulterous yearnings: *"...I have a few things against you, because you allow that woman Jezebel...to teach and seduce My servant to*

*commit sexual immorality...Indeed I will cast her into a
sickbed, and those who commit adultery with her into
great tribulation, unless they repent of their deeds...all the
churches shall know that I am He who searches the minds
and hearts. And I will give to each one of you according to
your works"* (Rev. 2:20-23).

The promise of "great tribulation" happens to fall
within verse 22, equating to "2:22." Many prophetic voices
in recent years have approached me with their experience
of seeing the numbers "222" very often about them, and
asking my thoughts as to what this may mean. In short,
and as is typical, I remind them that they are the
figurative eyes of the Body of Christ, as such their eyes
will be repeatedly attacked by lust, eroticism, and
pornographic images—to obscure their vision. I then
underscore the re-reading of Revelation 2:22, that they
may in turn allow the Holy Spirit to burn this warning
into their hearts. I then supplement this warning with my
brutally honest story about my failure to heed the same.
Once the full gravity of my story settles upon them, they
are typically met with such unrelenting conviction that
they soon find themselves dully purged.

There are other significant "222" references in
scripture; one of which I have alluded to in other writings;
however within the context of this book, may the warning
found in Revelation 2:22, and its pointed contemporary
application therein find its way into the harbor of your
soul as well.

The word "hour" in scripture is very often figurative
of that which denotes a point in history, whether past, or
that which is yet to be written—the future. With this
understanding in view, I believe it timely to allude also to
Revelation 3:10 which speaks of *"...the hour of trial which
shall come upon the whole world, to test those who dwell
on earth."* Irrespective of what theologians may insist
upon otherwise, we have at this stage entered this very
"hour of trial," globally. During this trial, everything
within our frames that is counter to God's perfect will for
our lives will meet with gnawing conviction—conviction
induced by the Holy Spirit, Who is not very agreeable to

sharing His residency in your heart, mind, body, soul and spirit. Believers who yet insist upon dual-occupancy will become increasingly more miserable as the result of the mounting internal combustion. The Lord prefers that we are rather hot or cold, but to persist upon prolonged compromise (luke-warmness) is a dangerous place for the Believer. As we are rather obedient to the course of these convictions by yielding ourselves to ongoing purging, we will further conform to Christ-likeness, and therein find the grace to whither what is now upon us.

As we then consider our personal trials and subsequent purging, consider also for a moment that in 2013 there were 2,123 known incidents of Christian martyrdom around the globe, which is nearly double the number known of 2012. These statistics do not account for the unknown death toll of Believers within the brutal prisons of North Korea, which, if known, could very well double or even *triple* this number. For those of us in the West; we must ready ourselves for life-threatening persecution; a reality which is presently being fostered by our very government.

For the moment, lets resume our brief meditation of Revelation 2:22, by suggesting that the Apologists among us have found the *perfect* entrance through which to discount the sobering implications of the aforementioned "sickbed" excerpt; as "*surely this word to the Church in Thyatira was meant only for the Church in Thyatira*"; which therefore places me, the writer, *"guilty of taking scripture out of context,"* and breaking the laws of hermeneutics (the formal *soft-science* of interpreting scripture). To this sentiment, allow me to say candidly that I am very much aware of the tenets of hermeneutics (my gluteus medius and spine have endured *thousands* of hours on hard wooden and plastic seats in bible colleges and seminary). However, I am *more so* aware of how God in His omnipresence and omnipotence has spoken countless words to His saints—words that, though spoken and written thousands of years ago, are equally applicable to His saints *today*. Much of the Book of Revelation holds prophetic allegory which speaks *precisely* to the age (the "hour") in which we now live—despite the fact that it was initially spoken directly to the Church in Thyatira in this example, somewhere between A.D. 70 and A.D. 95.

The foundation of theological study does well to maintain the following 3-part approach to interpreting a given excerpt of scripture: 1) What does it say, literally? 2) What did it mean, to whom it was said, at the time? And, 3) What does it mean to me, today? Let us hereafter meditate upon what it means to *us—today*. The relevance of its historicity, by contrast, is quickly fading, much to the dismay of my dear exegete friends. Exposition, or, the rubber-meets-the-road-life-application has risen to the place of extreme importance in this hour.

To those of you who would have rather not taken this brief detour into theological banter; allow me to divulge that I must deal with theological monkeys on a near-daily basis. The formal study of theology has spawned monstrous streams of "thinkers" who take it upon themselves to utterly destroy anything spoken or written which bears testament to personal revelation or personal experience with the *God* of revelation. Assuming my theological bug spray has repelled these monkeys for the moment, I continue...

"Behold then, the kindness and the severity of God...," reads Romans 11:22. This verse was spoken in the context of one of several vital excerpts of scripture which substantiate and define the "one new man" spoken of in scripture (i.e., the ultimate marriage of Jew and Gentile—in Christ). In the context of my allusion to verse 22 of Romans 11, I am emphasizing that scripture underscores *both* God's kindness *and* His severity. Christians are not exempt from God's severity—especially those who've been groomed, honed and molded into vessels of leadership, and who subsequently influence significant numbers of people. To further underscore my point herein, is to also quote King Solomon in Proverbs 29:1, which reads: *"A man who hardens his neck after much reproof will suddenly be broken beyond remedy."* To this end, I will confess to you dear reader, that I have felt

"broken beyond remedy" for over 13 years, as the result of the tinnitus condition which plagues me; for such there is no known medical cure to date. I have been forgiven and cleansed of my sin, yet I have bore the deep scar of my sin for many years, in the form of hideous psychological and emotional torment spawned by such.

Having searched my soul for over a decade at this stage, and having submitted myself to every conceivable flavor of healing and deliverance ministry, I have yet, as the result of much fasting and prayer, met with God's continual empowerment to speak-into the lives of many people in and through my brutally honest testimony. My honesty very often disarms those who have found themselves in bondage similar to the bondage I have walked in. This disarming-dynamic has enabled me to speak deeply into the lives of a sea of people, permitting me to watch God's marvelous grace break chains of bondage, and set people free, through deliverance from the same. I share this as a word of encouragement to you, should you as well find yourself continually swathing a path through the debris, clutter and carnage of the fruits of your disobedience.

Though I am convinced that God has shown me His severity, by allowing the severity of the tinnitus to torment me for so long, I am equally convinced that He has shown me His *kindness*—adorning the pages of scripture—His kindness which includes His desire that everyone suffering sickness and disease and torment meet with healing and wholeness. It is for this reason that I petition the Throne Room daily, for my healing. As I do so, I approach Him in a posture of deep *teshuvah,* believing that in due season I will be free of this affliction, whereas daily I stand upon 1 Peter 2:24-25 (and so should you), which reads: *"...He Himself bore our sins in His body upon the cross...for by His wounds you were healed...the Shepherd and Guardian of your souls."*

***

Psalm 91:15

"He shall call upon Me, and I will answer him; I will be with him in trouble; I will deliver him and honor him."

As we call upon the Lord in every circumstance, He ultimately answers us—often in ways which defy our predisposed paradigm. Very often His answer comes in the form of a message *within* our very circumstances. Other times, His answer comes in very subtle and often humorous ways long after the dust has settled. Sometimes He delivers us immediately from our circumstances. His deliverance comes in a variety of ways, and it is often followed by Him raising us up yet again and placing us back on the saddle of the work He has given us to do—in His name.

On the surface, and with cartoon-like imagery as I often imagine such myself, we can recall the messes we've woven about ourselves. Once we've created the mess, we beg God to deliver us from it. Often times He does. But then why would He go on to endorse us thereafter, after we have made complete fools of ourselves? I believe the answer lay in our heart-posture as we approach Him. For as we humble ourselves in a posture of contrition and brokenness, whether figuratively or literally lying prostrate before Him (it is our heart condition which matters most), He lifts us up again—He under-girds us and endorses us, yet again. James 4:10 reads accordingly, *"Humble yourselves in the presence of the Lord, and He will exalt you."*

For over three decades at this stage, even while in the midst of creating relational carnage, wounding others and wobbling about in a spirit of delusion—not unlike the old string-pulled tops that begin to wobble as they slow to a stop and then topple over; I have sought to establish a time-window within each day, to sit in stillness and in silence, to hear the voice of God. Very often it has not been until days or weeks later, that I see His fingerprints in my circumstances, and when I do, I am often quickened and reminded that I've seen His fingerprints because I have stilled myself—having conditioned myself *to practice His presence.* In and through practicing His presence, He has steadily guided me into layer-upon-layer of deliverance and healing. Equally so, He has shown me layer-upon-layer of revelation of what is unfolding around me—a panoramic perspective about me, and a linear perspective looking forward; which sees-out over the battlefield and into what lay ahead.

  For the longest time I had convinced myself that what I was "seeing" was a combination of delusion and brain damage from my drug-infested years as a teen. It was not then until a steady stream of substantial leaders began to affirm what I was seeing, that I realized the Lord had gifted me to "see" things, much like a person sitting upon a very high wall, which permits one to see more deeply into the horizon at what lay ahead. Having realized and accepted the fact that I have been placed upon a wall for this purpose, I have sought to exercise as much sensitivity and discernment as I am able, to understand the timing of the sharing of what I see. Irrespective, I have been met with perpetual rejection by the masses as I have shared what I "see." Rejection therefore has become a way of life for me, as a watchman. Its sting can be devastating, as the sting often goes deep—into the rejection-wound that I have carried all of my life. As the result, and on countless occasions, I have climbed down from the "wall" and have told the Lord that I'm tired of "seeing," as every time I share what I see, the multitudes curse me. On countless occasions I have sought to resign my post. In these moments God has raised up unsuspecting voices to wholly confirm what I have shared. And it is for this reason that I carryon, in obedience, sharing what I do, and sharing more pointedly what you are now reading.

  Much of the Book of Revelation has remained a puzzling mystery for most. However I believe that grace is being poured-out upon all who would choose to meditate on such in this hour; but not only grace; *blessing* as well. The book declares that we will be blessed for simply reading it. Equally so, I pray that you will be blessed by my brief meditation of Revelation 16:15, which reads,

"Behold, I am coming like a thief. Blessed is the one who stays awake and keeps his clothes, so that he will not walk about naked and men will not see his shame." For as we have considered earlier, that much of scripture (especially the Book of Revelation) which relates to the End Times has been penned with allegory, metaphor and symbolism; it can equally be said that much of the same is quite *literal*. In fact, one of my favorite theologians (I don't have many favorites in this department I will add) has stated: *"When meditating upon scripture; when the plain sense makes sense, seek no other sense, or you might very well wind up with <u>non</u>sense."* He is quite right.

Back to Revelation 16:15. Is it possible for us to "stay awake" perpetually? Certainly not. What therefore did Jesus mean, by suggesting that we "stay awake"? He is referring to our *spiritual* sobriety. He is calling us to remain "awake" spiritually, perpetually, and to refuse to allow our spiritual antennae to be pushed back into the retracted position. We therefore stay awake in the manner in which Jesus implores us, by remaining in perpetual *communion* (intimacy) with Him—allowing no distraction to garner our devotion aside from complete devotion to Him; to be further conformed to His image; and to be further used as a conduit of His likeness in all that we set our hands to.

How is it then that we are also to "keep our clothes"? Are we to go to bed fully dressed in the event our number is called while we're sleeping? Again, we must return to metaphor, as we "keep our clothes" by rather carefully guarding our *robes of righteousness* (i.e., Isaiah 61:10: *"...He has wrapped me with a robe of righteousness"...*). In Isaiah's day "righteousness" before God entailed that inclusive of keeping the law. In *our* day however, our righteousness is defined firstly in and through the Blood sacrifice of Jesus' atoning death on the Cross—and His subsequent resurrection. Though we are also implored and commanded to thereafter seek to live a righteous life, we cannot do so without perpetually failing. Jesus' atonement is therefore ongoing; for in addition to a one-time atonement for all of mankind, there is also His *ongoing* atoning work in our lives as we fall at His feet, confess our sins, and ask Him to cleanse us—over and over and over again.

Nestled *also* in "the back of the book," the Book of Revelation once again, is that found within the very last chapter—a key largely hidden from many Believer's in Jesus; hidden only because of the widespread disinterest in navigating the apparent theological jungle represented in the book. The "key" to which I refer, is not only a precious ruby nestled in a deep jungle, but also trampled upon and overlooked by men as they swath through the thick overgrowth of the jungle of life, while wiping their brows as they perspire profusely as the result of the taxing motion of their machetes. The "ruby" to which I refer is that of Revelation 22:14, which reads, *"Blessed are they who wash their robes, so that they may have the right to the tree of life, and may enter by the gates into the city."*

And the key herein is this, dear reader; the most literal translation of this verse, which is quite closely rendered above, denotes the *ongoing act* of washing our robes. Therefore, in order to have the right to the tree of life, we simply must wash our robes, each time we soil them. No matter how dirty we get them, and no matter how hopeless we feel as we see what appears to be permanent stains on our robes; Jesus is standing with open arms to receive us each time we confess our sin to Him and ask for His cleansing—by His blood.

Fulfilling our course in this life as a Believer in Jesus has never been defined by a one-time-transaction with Him—contrary to the belief within a significant (significant by size) branch of mainstream Christianity in the U.S., and which has been perpetuated for centuries at this stage. To the radical contrary, this erroneous theology is dispelled by one simple verse: *"...it is the one who endures to the end, who shall be saved"* (Matthew 10:22b). Our right to the tree of life therefore, my friend, is but a matter of enduring, and we endure by daily washing our robes—it is *that* simple—simple enough for a child to understand. Perhaps this is why Jesus also told us in Mathew 18:3, that *"...unless you become as a little child, you will not see the kingdom."*

It is when our intellectual and theological snobbery becomes so muddled that a *child* cannot understand the core of its basis that we have sorely failed to embrace the simplicity of the gospel *ourselves*. As we remain like a child in our relationship to Jesus, we thereafter learn to recognize His embrace as we dare to crawl up and onto His lap, as we seek time with Him on a daily basis. This is the greatest ministry in which we will ever engage in this lifetime—that of ministry to *Him*. All else that we do in view of others, is but secondary.

Chapter Twelve

Like a Weaned Child
גמול ילד כמו

For as far back as I can remember into my childhood, and through present day, I have sought to varying degrees, to convince others that I am someone else, as I have been terrified of being rejected for what I am, who I was created to be. I recall my elementary years in school, consumed in fear and made to feel stupid; laughed at, scorned, threatened, and very alone. I yet recall sometime around the 3rd or 4th grade, immersing myself in the study of birds. I believe it began during a "free reading period," when I opened a picture book of birds. For months thereafter it seems, one particular teacher, perhaps my homeroom teacher, allowed me to spend much of my time immersed in birds. I recall drawing, coloring, cutting-out and taping them to my desk in upright positions. It is clear as I look back to that brief period in school, that my fixation upon birds was two-fold: they were delicate, gentle creatures, which reflected what was being destroyed or threatened in me; and yet they were removed from all threats and turmoil below, as they flew into the heavens with grace, ease, and freedom. For this brief period I dropped my guard while at school, and had become so focused upon birds that it matter not what others were doing and saying about me. The few years that I can vaguely recall prior to this brief season, and the many years that I can more vividly recall thereafter; were characterized by a safety-mask, carefully crafted to shield my very sensitive and wounded core.

Many of us walk in seasons of "dryness" and spiritual barrenness, all the while believing that *"God is simply taking me back to the desert for a while, to help me to go deeper."* At times this is the case. Equally so however, at times it is because we have insisted upon clinging with all our might, to a mask that we hope to convince others *is* who we are. As we remain hidden behind such the mask, we unknowingly place a barrier between ourselves and the gentle voice and prodding of the Holy Spirit—Who with great care, seeks to mold us into a greater likeness of Jesus with each day. As we willfully forge ahead ignoring His gentle tugging, He may lift His hand of grace from our lives, enabling everything we touch to topple over, thus forcing us to our knees in despair, that we might again cry-out to Him for His renewed presence. On our knees, at this stage, is *precisely* where He wants us; it is hereafter that He can begin to speak to our condition and resume His gentle molding; as on our knees we've no opportunity to run, nor to busy ourselves with vain activities which distract us from acknowledging His still, small voice which steadily prods us, and whispers to our souls the need to come clean.

As we exude such behavior, we are collectively emulating much of what the Body of Christ universal is being severely judged for in this hour, especially so in this country. We have allowed a mounting epidemic of showmanship, soulish charisma and terminal religious charades to consume the Church in the West, effectively masking our pitiful state. For such, it is time to walk-out *teshuvah*, and to lay this taxing charade to rest. And it *really is* taxing; it takes a great deal of energy to manufacture enough of a false self to convince others that we are someone we are not. When we are able to deal the deathblow to this phantom, we are so much more relaxed and at-peace with ourselves and others. It is in this posture that the Holy Spirit freely moves through us with grace, anointing and authority; this in stark contrast to the tremendous work involved in manufacturing soulish-hype before the masses.

A few years ago I was seated next to a very discerning brother in his living room. We were recovering

(in a good way) from a few days of very intense ministry—
intense also in a good way. He turned his TV on and went
to a Christian TV station, where we caught mid-stream a
message being delivered by an internationally known
leader with a massive congregation. Maybe 60 seconds
into our viewing of this message, my friend turned to me
and said, *"Do you see anything wrong with this picture?"* I
laughed, as I had seen precisely what he had seen. I
replied, *"Yes, he's working too hard."* He was perspiring
from the soulish labor involved in stirring up superficial
hyper-emotionalism, and in so doing was convincing the
10's of 1000's of attendees that he was really going
somewhere with his message, when in fact he was going
nowhere. Something was very, very wrong, and it was
simply saddening to watch. I couldn't watch anymore of
it. Within moments I was given a word of knowledge—
crystal clear—about what it was that was preventing the
Holy Spirit from anointing his message. Was the word of
knowledge that for my personal entertainment—as many
moving within prophetic circles preclude? Hardly, it was
that I might immediately intercede for my brother's
nakedness. Very often what the Holy Spirit shows us
about others, is that not for the purposes of responding
with high-brow judgment and actuating a slander-
campaign, but much rather to simply *intercede*, to *pray*
for the afflicted soul. He reveals things to us because He
entrusts us—to pray. The more we choose contrary
responses, the more He will reduce the steady stream of
revelation flowing to us and through us.

The issue remains however, that a man speaking to
10's of 1000s of people, as well as commanding the
television sets and laptops of millions of people, has
chosen a phantom-self through which to perform on a
Sunday morning. I'm inclined to quip that I could not
imagine his internal misery during the televised service.
Admittedly however, I *can* imagine his misery, as I've
welcomed and harbored the very same.

For many centuries, and perhaps even more
pointedly so in this century, Believers have wondered
what Jesus really meant when He said, *"...My yoke is easy*

133

and my burden is light." The Greek word for "yoke" is ZYGOS (Ζυγός), the definition of which includes metaphor for "any burden or point of bondage." Jesus implores us in Mathew 11:29, *"Take My yoke upon you and learn from Me, for I am gentle and humble in heart, and you will find rest for your souls."* The key herein to understanding what it means to take His yoke, is that which is in essence "hidden in plain sight" within this verse. For it is gentleness and humility of heart, which fosters Jesus' yoke upon our lives. It is when we allow the stressors, pressures and soulish lures of the work of ministry to override and supplant the gentleness and humility of heart within Jesus, and that which He has deposited in us, that we take-on a yoke of slavery to our carnality; wherein we succumb to vain impulses and allow ourselves to be governed by the expectations of others.

I am convinced at this stage that the *fullness* of Jesus' "yoke" is that of His complete license to govern the breadth and depth of our hearts—as we press-in to ongoing intimacy with Him. When we are then yoked to ongoing intimacy with Him, leaving our falsehoods and denials behind, His subsequent hand upon us reveals His unmistakable fingerprints as we are used as an authentic vessel in the work of the ministry—which then flows with relative ease, and with little soulish work on our part.

As we run into the arms of Jesus—and this is really much easier than we realize—because His arms are *always* open—we open ourselves up to receiving an authentic dose of His very tangible mercy, as so beautifully described by David in Psalm 103:2-14: *"Bless the Lord, O my soul...Who forgives all your iniquities, Who heals all your diseases...the Lord is merciful and gracious, slow to anger and abounding in mercy. He will not always strive with us, nor will He keep His anger forever. He has not dealt with us according to our sins, nor punished us according to our iniquities. For as the heavens are high above the earth, so great is His mercy toward those who fear Him; as far as the east is from the west, so far has He removed our transgressions from us. As a father pities his children, so the Lord pities those who fear Him. For He knows our frame; He remembers that we are dust."*

This profound excerpt of Psalm 103, says in rubber-meets-the-road terms (i.e., paraphrased): *"God knows precisely who you are. He knows your frailties and your secret-sins. But He does not meet-out His awesome recompense as He should, when we simply purpose to fear Him, by acknowledging and revering His majesty, by prostrating ourselves before Him in repentance. As we do this, our sins are erased."* And they are erased by the atoning Blood of Jesus. It can be said that we are all "a work in progress." We never truly "arrive" at perfection in this lifetime—perfection, as we understand it. I believe the only exception to this statement is that which occurs moments before we meet Him; the final moments on our deathbeds, when His angelic host draws near to us and gives us a glimpse of just how close He really is. It is in those final moments, when we behold His glory, that our hearts return a state of purity not unlike our infancy; undefiled by a life-long struggle with the works of darkness. In this state, our final moments on earth represent what I believe to be "perfection."

There are many excerpts of scripture that speak of perfection. One of these is James 1:14, which reads: *"...let endurance have its perfect result, so that you may be perfect and complete, lacking in nothing."* The Greek word for "perfect" (*teleios*), means among other things, *"the consummation of human integrity and virtue."* It also means, *"to be brought to an end."* And in our final moments on earth; for those who have embraced the Lordship of Jesus; our striving is brought to an end, and we reach the momentary apex of human integrity and virtue—by beholding the majesty of the Lord—as we also behold the vastness of our frailties and vanity, as the result.

Having spent countless occasions with those in the final moments of their lives; and that primarily with those who have embraced the Lordship of Jesus; I have observed in the span of but a few days; sometimes the span of but a few hours; a glorious transition from initially being utterly consumed with grief as they look back upon their failures and sins; to being utterly consumed by the peace of God as He begins to draw nearer than ever, and makes the reality of heaven known.

We do not have to wait until the very "end" however, to behold such a measure of the Lord's majesty that we also become aware of the vastness of our frailties and vanities, like those on their deathbeds. For as we so press-in to know Him with each day, we are very often granted glimpses of His glory—just enough of a glimpse to effect the ongoing purging required to make a little more room for His transformative work in our lives. Many of us have been robbed of this liberty, by the devastating sting of *religion*—a brand of Christianity which harbors legalism at its core, and which keeps the subscriber in a perpetual state of feeling accused, scorned and condemned. Barring what could become a lengthy discourse on Demonology; I will rather simply say that the Religious Spirit (I address him by name) is responsible for more of our collective defunct spiritual state, than any other spiritual entity or dynamic.

I recall like it was yesterday, some twenty years ago listening to a "pastor" tell me that because of the things I had been exposed to while young, and because of how I had subsequently lived-out a life of extreme dysfunction and sin; I was destined to be used in the End-Times as an agent of the Adversary, to cause others to sin; and that I had reached a state of being unredeemable. This man's comments devastated me, and nearly crippled me for a number of years. He had wholly discounted the power of the Blood of Jesus to restore a ravaged human being to a place of healing, peace, and fruitfulness thereafter. It took me a number of years to later recognize the *spirit* behind the man who had so thoroughly condemned me. I readily recognize it now, and almost daily engage a dragon-slaying match in this regard wherever I go.

How is it that I would allow such a negative element to creep-into the closing chapter of my book? Sometimes we cannot fully appreciate the value of a warm breeze until we've first spent a few moments shivering in the cold. Allow me therefore to offer you a "warm breeze," by way of the reminder that there are no depths to which you can fall in this lifetime, as a Believer, where you will not also find the arms of Jesus reaching for you—as you humble yourself, approach Him with a contrite heart, repent, and ask Him for forgiveness and restoration. *That* is the "gospel truth," my friend.

It was before the advent of our Savior that God equally responded to authentic *teshuvah*, and offered healing and restoration. That we have been afforded a New Covenant, which not only restores us to Him, but also wipes away our every stain, is beyond what our finite minds can fully grasp. It is therefore much easier to simply come to Him as a little child (Matt. 18:3), and receive the reality of His forgiveness, cleansing, healing and restoration, by *faith*—the same faith that Abraham exercised.

There are times when, as I still myself, the raging of the piercing squeal in my head (Tinnitus) is mentally and emotionally crippling. To exacerbate the experience, often times at the very *same* time I am deeply saddened as I reflect upon those I've wounded by my dysfunctions and demonic strongholds, especially my children. The collective loss of life that I have caused is staggering. It is in these moments that I remind myself that the Lord does not accuse nor condemn those that are His. He will, through His Holy Spirit, convict us ongoing, but He simply does not accuse and condemn. The primary medium through which I break-free from such the oppressive attack, is that of *worshipping* Him. Our primary job descriptions as we transition to our glorified state, will be that of worshipping the Lamb on the Throne. The apex of our ministry therefore, and that irrespective of what others or we call ourselves at this stage in the work of the ministry; is that of *worship*.

As our planet spins more rapidly into world-chaos and inches ever-closer to fulfilling the cataclysmic eschatological time-tables written upon the fabric of the Nation of Israel, each of us will be prodded, tugged-at, nudged and wooed into more deeply worshipping the Lion of the Tribe of Judah—in and through our personal

137

lives—and in and through the public adoration of Him as
we congregate en masse. I therefore suggest we ready
ourselves for an eternity of so doing, by submitting
ourselves to the immediate practice herein.

As a child raises its arms skyward, in a gesture of
longing to be picked up and embraced, so does a
Heavenly Father receive us as we lift our hands toward
Him, longing for His embrace. He sits patiently, in a
timeless posture, gazing upon us with omniscience and
all knowing. I do not doubt that we amuse Him often, as
we scurry about, doing our best to cover our tracks while
also seeking to make sense of what we're called to do.
Along the way He often inserts subtle hints as to where
we should place our feet, and what we should be doing
with our hands. And as He does, I do not doubt that we
often resemble children who have been given paints and
brushes, and have been placed on a massive canvas, left
to our own devices. We can thereafter paint quite a mess
of our lives. As we do so I do not doubt that we often
amuse Him and even make Him laugh. And, at times, I do
not doubt that we sadden Him. But in the end, He
possesses the omnipotence to turn the canvas of our lives
into a beautiful portrait of salvation, healing and
deliverance—not only for ourselves—but also for the
multitudes we have been granted privilege to impact along
the way.

***

Psalm 131:2

*"Surely I have composed and quieted my soul;
like a weaned child rests against his mother,
my soul is like a weaned child within me."*

Toward the latter end of King David's life it became
increasingly clear that he was given the grace to see
glimpses of the very heart of God—as it is—not as we
perceive it to be. Thereafter David met with the grace to
embrace God, as a child would rest against his mother.

For over 33 years at this stage, I have observed the ebb and flow of the Holy Spirit's unique seasons of movement within the Church at large. One of the more colorful seasons has been that evidenced by authentic prophetic ministry returning to the heartbeat of public gatherings, in the form of a resurgence and a refinement of the gift and the ministry in general. As multitudes have clamored to find their place within the prophetic stream, equal multitudes have met with dismay and disillusionment as the result of mass-perversions and distortions within the gift and ministry. It stands to reason, that evil would weave its way into an authentic and strategic move of the Holy Spirit. After all, prophetic ministry exposes demonic strategies. Of course then, the hordes of hell would seek to destroy it. What I wish that I could convey to every soul who has been wounded by misappropriations of the gift, and the ministry in general; is that those who speak the oracles of God are those who have been weaned of selfish positioning and posturing, and who have learned to embrace the Lord in intimacy not unlike a child resting against their mother. For it is in this posture of intimacy, that we learn to hear the heartbeat of God. The more we hear His heartbeat, the more we understand His heartbeat for *us*. As well, the more we understand His heartbeat for us, the more we may with grace speak His heartbeat for *others*—the essence of prophetic ministry.

I have spoken of the "full-circle" experience within the cycle of our lives, wherein, as the result of our dependence upon God, we return to childlikeness as we draw very near the end of our assignment on earth. We are born into relative purity as infants, and we die in relative purity as we continue to embrace the Lordship of Jesus deep within our hearts, into our final moments of life. As I consider this cycle, I have often pondered why it is that we cannot rather experience this return to purity much sooner in our adult lives, than to rather experience such on our deathbeds. I have concluded that it is because of our relative incapacitation in the final moments, that in turn leaves us wholly vulnerable to

139

God's arrest of our souls. At this stage we have ceased striving, and we are able to fully *"know* [behold] *God"* (Ps. 46:10).

Our waking hours as adults are met with the ongoing propensity for strife. We meet with such through two avenues; that which the works of evil seeks to throw at us, and that which we create for ourselves, in and of our own doing. It is rare that we fully negotiate and navigate the art of entering into God's rest. His rest is much more expansive than that of our physical posture in reclining; His rest is a way of life, wherein irrespective of what we are doing from moment to moment He can yet still the turbulent waters of our soul, and calm the potential storm of thoughts and emotions. The measure of peace we experience with Him is directly commensurate to the degree to which we will purpose to align every facet of our lives with His will. Again, I refer to peace *within*, and that irrespective of our circumstances without.

Many of the early mystics were terribly misunderstood. Though some spent their lives seeking to portray the life of a spiritual being so far removed from the common man that they were untouchable; many had simply experienced so much of God's tangible presence that all they wanted to do thereafter was that to bask in His presence, and spend their lives in prayer—praying that all of mankind would also discover precious jewels through intimacy with Him—jewels sitting just beneath the goads in the road, over which we often trip as we stumble about in a confused and exhausted religious stupor.

One such mystic who found a precious treasure chest of intimacy with God, was that of the French Madame Jeanne Guyon (1648—1717), known widely in her time as an advocate of *Quietism.* Much more than an advocate however, she embodied the core principle of such, as her life was a perpetual demonstration of quietness and stillness before the Lord—a posture of the heightened awareness of His presence everywhere, and at all times. Madame Guyon suffered terribly in her lifetime, through abuses from family members; widowhood at age

28, and extended imprisonment thereafter for allegedly promoting heresy. My study of Jeanne Guyon's life, as well as the study of the lives of many other saints who have gone before us in relative contemporary history, has convinced me that we cannot remove ourselves from suffering. After all, Jesus Himself said, *"...in this world you will have tribulation"* (John 16:33). We can however press-in to know God with such intimacy that all that unfolds about us in the days ahead simply cannot shake us from the perpetual knowledge of the nearness of His love, His grace, His mercy, His compassion, and His *kindness.*

The preeminent apostle Paul spoke of a daily death to his flesh (*"...I die daily,"* I Cor. 15:31). In like manner, our task in this life, as a Believer, is that to die daily to the internal war within us that seeks to prevent us from fulfilling the breadth of what each of us has been gifted to accomplish. And it is in and through *teshuvah,* a turning-away from that which defiles, and a *return-to* the loving embrace of Jesus, that we will, through subsequent cleansing and renewal, gracefully fulfill all that has been set before us to accomplish; as individuals, and as His Bride collectively.

"Repent and return, so that your sins may be wiped away, in order that times of refreshing may come from the presence of the Lord;" (Acts 3:19).

Epilogue

It is my sincere hope that at this stage, it is very clear that my impetus for writing this brutally honest biographical sketch was *anything but* that rooted in an attempt to position and posture myself for the purpose of cultivating more opportunity for "public ministry." In what I suspect will be the opposite; I must believe that as the result of my story, many, perhaps multitudes, will find it difficult to conceive of me furthering the work of the ministry. If there was therefore, any potential for selling myself in the work of the ministry, it was dully placed upon an altar of sacrifice as I began telling my story herein.

My great joy in life to date, has been that while speaking-into the Body of Christ at large, and experiencing the awesome power of His Holy Spirit at work in healing very broken hearts—including mine— each time I tell my story. Though I do very much harbor a deeply heartfelt desire to share my message abroad, and within any venue that would opt to host me for such; I yet feel challenged to remain content in knowing that the circulation of the book alone will touch hearts, and will motivate the same to adopt a heart of contrition, and carry out the authentic work of *teshuvah.* And as we do so collectively prostrate ourselves before God and repent for lives of luke-warmness and compromise, I believe He will raise us up to ultimately walk in the greatest level and measure of His anointing and authority witnessed in contemporary Church history.

I thank my Father and Mother for giving me life; I thank my Heavenly Father for offering me *new life,* over and over again; and I thank my wife Gigi for the kindness, compassion, mercy and love she demonstrates to me daily. For as she does so, she so emulates Jesus that I am reminded of just how close He really is.

www.TeshuvahTzion.org